The Ordination of a Priest:

Reflections on the Priesthood in the Rite of Ordination

by Rev. Mark O'Keefe, OSB

Foreword by Archbishop Daniel Buechlein, OSB, DD

© 1999
Saint Meinrad School of Theology
ISBN 0-87029-326-5
Printed at Abbey Press
St. Meinrad, IN 47577

TABLE OF CONTENTS

Foreword

This second inspiring book on the ministerial priesthood by Fr. Mark O'Keefe, OSB, is a natural sequence that builds on the first, *In Persona Christi: Reflections on Priestly Identity and Holiness*. In his previous set of reflections, Fr. Mark provided new clarity in understanding the contemporary concept of the ministerial priesthood in the documents of the Second Vatican Council as well as in Pope John Paul II's landmark Apostolic Letter, *Pastores Dabo Vobis*. He also sketched an inspiring path to priestly holiness. In this second set of reflections, while shedding even more light on the distinctive identity and meaning of the sacrament of Holy Orders, he achieves an even greater and refreshing level of inspiration for the pursuit of holiness in priestly ministry.

The Ordination of a Priest: Reflections on the Priesthood in the Rite of Ordination provides a contemporary commentary on the ancient rite of ordination while it also draws out new meaning. The focus is contemporary, yet the reflections extract the richest inspirational dimensions of the apostolic tradition of the rite.

These reflections are also practical. For example, Fr. Mark stresses the realistic challenge of proclaiming the Word of God day in and day out. His charism and strong convictions as a seminary rector are appropriately prominent in his repeated stress on the priority of preparing the homily for Eucharist. He provides thoughtful reflection on the multifaceted relationship of priests and bishops in the local and universal Church. He addresses the sometimes thorny issue of obedience in a democratic and egalitarian milieu. He provides helpful advice in understanding and also addressing the contemporary challenge of forging an "inter-generational" fraternity among priests.

Throughout these reflections, there is a stress on the spiritual and sanctifying dimensions of priestly ministry as understood both in word and ritual symbolism in the very rite of ordination. Perhaps the most powerful contribution of this timely work is the consistent and no-nonsense emphasis on the essential challenge of spiritual development in priestly ministry. The reflections on "the priest in prayer" are moving.

I couldn't think of a better companion for a seminarian while on retreat in preparation for ordination to the diaconate and ordination to the priesthood than these reflections. I couldn't think of a better companion for a priest or bishop while making his annual spiritual retreat. Nor could I think of a more enriching source for new gratitude and refreshing zeal as a priest or bishop celebrates the anniversary of his ordination.

+ Daniel M. Buechlein, OSB
Archbishop of Indianapolis

Acknowledgements

Early in developing my own reflections on the rite of ordination, Fr. Kurt Stasiak, OSB, associate professor of sacramental theology, offered insights from his area of expertise and suggestions for further reading. He later read the text and offered further comment. I am grateful for his assistance. Archabbot Lambert Reilly, OSB, and Msgr. Jerry Neufelder, assistant professor of spirituality, also offered helpful comments after reading a draft of the book. I am grateful to them as well.

Archbishop Daniel Buechlein has once again honored me by reading a draft of my work and writing the Foreword for the finished product. In fact, he should recognize a number of the insights in this book as his own, since I learned them from listening to his ordination homilies over the last several years, here at Saint Meinrad and at his Cathedral in Indianapolis.

I offered some of my reflections to a small group of my brother priests who were on retreat at Saint Meinrad. I learned from their reactions and comments.

I want to thank Mrs. Barbara Crawford for serving as editor for my book and seeing it through the publication process. All of this is in addition to the fine work that she does as director of communications for Saint Meinrad, ably assisted by Mrs. Mary Jeanne Schumacher and Ms. Jo Rita Brahm. Mrs. Marilyn Brahm, my executive secretary, has assisted with some of the details of preparing the final text. As secretary to the president-rector since Archbishop Buechlein's first year as president-rector of Saint Meinrad School of Theology in 1971, she has made considerable contributions to the priestly formation program at Saint Meinrad.

Finally, I want to express my thanks and admiration for the men who are presently preparing for the priesthood at Saint Meinrad and those whom I have had the privilege of teaching and directing over the last 12 years. Their dedication to priestly ministry, the depth of their faith, and their generous self-giving to the Lord in the service of his people are a constant challenge to me to be a better pastor to them, a better priest for them, a better teacher about the meaning of this awesome vocation to which we have been so wonderfully called. I thank them, and I thank God for them.

List of Abbreviations

Documents of the Second Vatican Council:

LG   *Lumen Gentium* (Dogmatic Constitution
on the Church)

PO   *Presbyterorum Ordinis* (Decree on the
Ministry and Life of Priests)

SC   *Sacrosanctum Concilium* (Constitution on
the Sacred Liturgy)

Writings of Pope John Paul II:

PDV   *Pastores Dabo Vobis* (I Will Give You
Shepherds)

Holy Thursday   *Letters to My Brother Priests: Holy
Thursday* (1979-91). Chicago: Midwest
Theological Forum, 1992.

Document by the Congregation for the Clergy:

Directory   *Directory for the Life and Ministry of Priests*
(1994)

Committee on Priestly Life and Ministry, National Conference of Catholic Bishops

FIYH   *Fulfilled in Your Hearing: The Homily in the
Sunday Assembly* (1982)

Introduction

Lex Orandi, Lex Credendi

Lex orandi, lex credendi. The law of prayer is the law of belief. What the Christian community does at the liturgy reveals many of its core beliefs. Liturgical actions and the words spoken by the community in the context of its common worship, as these have developed over a long tradition and as defined by the Church's authority, disclose commonly held (if rarely articulated) beliefs. And those who participate in the liturgy are subsequently formed, often unconsciously but powerfully, by the actions they perform and witness and by the words that they say.

Some of the fundamentals of the Christian faith are manifest, for example, in the celebration of the Eucharist. The simple fact that people of different classes, races, genders, and ages gather at one table, to share one bread and one cup, reveals a fundamental belief about the basic equality of all people, about our relationship to one another as brothers and sisters, and about our hope for a future when all that separates us from one another will be destroyed. Our belief that the Lord is truly present in ordinary bread and wine, broken and poured out, discloses our most fundamental Christian beliefs about the goodness of creation, about the incarnation of the Son of God in ordinary human flesh, about the shape of the salvation he accomplished through his own body broken and his own blood poured out, and about the consequent shape of the lives of those who would follow this Lord through eating the bread and drinking from the cup.

Lex orandi, lex credendi. Reflection on the words and actions of the Church's rite of ordination to the priesthood can yield a better understanding of the meaning of the priesthood and, I trust, for priests and priesthood candidates, a deeper appropriation of the priesthood in their own lives. The essential elements of the rite come down to us from the early Church, most notably the laying on of hands. While there have been various adaptations throughout the centuries, the basic elements of the rite reveal a deep sense of the Church's understanding of ordained ministry to God's people.

In the course of this book, I offer my own reflections on the priesthood as the rite reveals the meaning of this awesome vocation precisely in the hope that I can help priests and seminarians to attain a better appropriation of the life and ministry to which we are called. As Cardinal Basil Hume has suggested, reviewing the rite of ordination can serve as an examination of conscience for the priest long after his own ordination (*Light in the Lord*, 42). Of course, priests themselves are not the only Catholics who can benefit from understanding the role of the ordained priesthood in the Church, and so I hope that these reflections might benefit other Catholics who attend ordinations, who work with priests and who wish to understand this distinctive calling within the Church.

What I want to offer in these pages is not so much a commentary that moves through the rite, examining each ritual action and the words that accompany them (though, in the course of my reflections, I will comment on all of the major actions and words of the rite). In fact, such a step-by-step commentary offered by an expert in liturgical theology would be very useful in fostering our reflection. Certainly, the history of the rite and the additions of various eras and cultures would offer a rich introduction to the different theological emphases of different times. I am, however, not a scholar of the liturgy nor of its history. I write as a priest, as one who has had the privilege of participating in many ordinations, and especially as a rector who oversees the formation of men for the day of their ordination and for the priestly life and ministry that follows.

My principal purpose, then, is to offer a reflection on the priesthood as the rite reveals it. I will enter into dialogue with the rite, bringing into the conversation the doctrinal understanding of the priesthood as papal and conciliar texts have defined it. In addition, the experience of living and ministering as a priest (my own experience, certainly, but also the experience of many other priests who minister in diverse contexts) informs my reflections.

Reading the rite of ordination together with the Second Vatican Council's *Decree on the Ministry and Life of Priests* (*Presbyterorum Ordinis*) makes evident that the 1968 reform of the rite of ordination followed closely the Council document. Perhaps this is most evident in the bishop's homily as it appears in the rite. Although the official text makes clear that the ordaining bishop is not required to use the "sample" homily in the rite, the themes and even the words of this sample homily follow the conciliar document so closely and are so consistent with the rest of the words of the rite that, in the course of my reflections, I will refer to the homily as part of the rite of ordination (see J.D. Crichton, *Christian Celebration: Understanding the Sacraments*, 152-53). In fact, in my experience, many bishops do use the provided homily, adapt it, or obviously use it as a basis for their own homilies.

The chapters which follow are not organized in the step-by-step order of the rite itself. Rather the reflections are addressed according to the themes suggested by *Presbyterorum Ordinis*: the nature of the priesthood (Chapter One); the threefold functions of the priest as a continuation of Christ's mission as Preacher/Teacher, Priest, and Shepherd (Chapters Two, Three and Four respectively); the priest's relations with bishops, brother priests, and the People of God (Chapters Five, Six and Seven respectively); and a final reflection on the priestly way of life (Chapter Eight). The presence of these conciliar themes in the rite of ordination will, I trust, become evident.

Those who have read my earlier reflection on priestly identity and holiness, *In Persona Christi: Reflections on Priestly Identity and Holiness*, will recognize familiar themes in this work. Certainly, this might be expected from an author writing two short books on similar topics. I trust, too, however, that the familiarity of the themes also reflects the consistency of the Church's understanding of the priesthood. In this current reflection on priesthood, through the lens of the rite of ordination, I hope to shed some further light on who and what a priest is called to be.

One

The Rite and the Nature of the Priesthood

The liturgy for the rite of ordination is almost always an impressive event, most especially for those who have never participated in an ordination before. Certainly, the large numbers of people assembled in a diocesan cathedral, the incense and processions, the beautiful music, the festive spirit—all of these experiences and more contribute to a sense that something very special is happening in the midst of this celebration. In fact, the ritual actions themselves and the accompanying words make this abundantly clear.

Many people comment, for example, on the powerful feelings invoked in them by the distinctive actions of ordination: the candidates prostrate on the floor while the assembly invokes what seems like the entire roll call of the saints; watching the bishop and priests, one by one, laying hands on the candidate in silence; watching as the new priest proudly takes on the vestments of his new office; seeing the newly ordained priest receiving the sign of peace from a long line of priests.

In fact, even without a close examination and reflection on the individual actions and words of the ordination rite, many things become clear from simply being present at an ordination liturgy. The Sacraments, as St. Augustine described them, are "visible words," that is, words that we see and experience and not only hear. Therefore, the experience of participating in the rite can make evident a number of important truths about the priesthood itself and the place of the priesthood within the life of the Church.

An Important Event in the Life of the Church

Perhaps most immediately, the ordination rite itself suggests that the action of ordaining a priest is a vitally important event for the life not only of the man being ordained, but of the Church itself. The introduction to the rite says: "The ordination of a priest should take place on a Sunday or a holyday, when a large number of the faithful can attend, unless pastoral reasons suggest another day." The space is to be arranged "so that the faithful may have a complete view of the liturgical rites."

The bishop, between two deacons, is preceded in procession by yet another deacon solemnly carrying the *Book of the Gospels* and a line of concelebrating priests. These introductory instructions to the rite, and most especially the distinctive ritual actions of the ordination, give an immediate sense that this action is an important event *of* the Church and an important event *for* the life of the Church.

Set Apart as a "Bearer of Mystery"

The rite of ordination discloses the fact that through ordination this new priest is being drawn into a realm of the sacred, the realm of mystery. Of course, throughout history, every religion in every culture has identified and set apart its "holy men or women," religious leaders who serve some mediating role between sacred and secular. In fact, Fr. Robert E. Barron has referred to the priest as a "bearer of mystery," a "mystagogue," who bears a transcendent mystery and initiates others into the mystery (Barron, 10). The very title *priest*, rather than *minister* or *pastor*, suggests this initiation of the ordinand into a life of "bearing mystery." And the distinctive actions of the rite build up this sense of mystery: the large number of vested ministers, the full prostration of the ordinand during the invocation of the saints, the laying on of hands in silence, the invocation of the Holy Spirit, the solemn Prayer of Consecration said over the kneeling ordinand, the investing of the new priest in the distinctive vesture of his sacred office, and the anointing with oil of hands that henceforth will bless, sanctify and consecrate.

The teaching of the Second Vatican Council and subsequent papal and curial documents clearly do want to move our thinking away from an earlier, almost exclusively cultic view of the priesthood. This move to a broader understanding of the priesthood, beyond viewing the priest only in a cultic, liturgical role, is evident in the words of the rite. My point here is simply to note that the actions of the ordination rite suggest powerfully that what is happening is not merely a commissioning of one minister among many, not merely an inauguration, not simply a special blessing. By participating in an ordination liturgy, one can perceive immediately that a man is being set apart in the sense of being consecrated for some special, profound and sacred service for the people assembled.

In fact, the actual experience of most priests will attest to the perception of sacred authority, divine mediation or "bearing of mystery" that accompanies their office. Wearing clerical attire in public often seems to evoke both respect and fascination in the people that one encounters (or, the opposite, a negative reaction that seems far out of proportion to whatever offense a priest's personal demeanor could usually evoke). Priests can often *feel* the unspoken expectation of the people that *he* is one who is set apart. Even when the priest enjoys warm relationships in a parish, he can continue to sense a different level of personal expectations from others and therefore the need for a more carefully monitored use of language, humor and behavior. (The sad reality of recent public scandals involving priests—and the combination of horror and fascination that the media manifests—also demonstrates the special, unspoken expectation that people have of priests.)

Perhaps some of this largely unarticulated sense of sacred authority can be explained by the process of being socialized into a Catholic culture in which priests are seen as set apart (though priests can also attest to similar reactions from non-Catholics). At the same time, however, whether they are conscious of it or not, people do long for an experience of the divine; and the priest symbolizes the transcendent for them. Priests can often sense that people view us as representatives of the divine, as bearers of mystery. We simply must become used to this reaction, even if we never become completely comfortable with it; adjusting to it is part of the transition the newly ordained must make. In sum, the experience of ordination rite reflects the lived experience of those who have been ordained.

Of course, the rite also simply reflects the fundamental reality of the priestly vocation. As the Council and subsequent papal documents have reaffirmed, the priest is "specially configured to Christ" as Head and Shepherd of the Church. Certainly, Christ Jesus is the one true mediator between God and humanity, between the divine and the human. However, the priests who act *in persona Christi capitis* (in the person of Christ as Head) share in this mediating role. The priest does not "mediate" between God and humanity as some kind of a "go-between." Rather, through the sacrament of Holy Orders, he makes Christ present through his life and ministry.

In fact, as Fr. Barron has suggested, the priest is a bearer of mystery. This is most apparent in his sacramental functioning, but it is also true in all of his priestly ministry. In the Eucharist, the priest stands in the place of Christ, calling Christ's people together, leading them in prayer, gathering their "spiritual sacrifice" into the all-sufficient self-giving of Christ to the Father. In his preaching, the priest speaks Christ's own Word, standing between the living Word of God and the living People of God. In the sacrament of Reconciliation, the priest mediates, makes present, the divine forgiveness of sinners.

The presence of transcendent mystery in the midst of the assembly of the flesh-and-blood People of God is not incidental to the rite of ordination. Nothing in the rite suggests that the newly ordained priest will be subjectively more holy than the people to whom he ministers (and lived experience would not bear out such a suggestion). But it is no accident that the rite suggests the incorporation of the ordinand into a new and sacred duty; it is no accident that the rite suggests that a man is being set apart, consecrated, for some special purpose in the Church. Through ordination, in fact, the Holy Spirit is specially configuring a man to act in the person of Christ as Head and Shepherd of the People of God.

Though he may not be more subjectively holy, a certain "objective holiness" can be said to be bestowed on the priest by ordination. He is consecrated, made holy for a holy purpose, specifically as a symbol of grace in and for the Church. Buildings, altars, chalices and other vessels are consecrated for their special use, made sacred for sacred purpose. Surely no less can be said for the priest configured to Christ to act in his name and in his person.

The challenge for the priest, especially for the newly ordained, is not to shrink from this reality. Rather, the priest must embrace it. Through the sacrament of Holy Orders and the outpouring of the Holy Spirit, he is specially configured to Christ to continue his mission; he is consecrated for servant-leadership of the People of God after the model of Jesus Christ. The priest will act on behalf of Christ (*in persona Christi*) and therefore he will act on behalf of Christ's Church (*in persona ecclesiae*). Even while embracing collaboration with others in ministry and while empowering lay people to take on their legitimate place and service in the Church, the priest cannot shrink from the sacred reality of his calling. The effectiveness of his priestly ministry—as well as his own sense of identity and purpose—depends on knowing who and what he has been called to be and to do.

At the same time, the priest must constantly remember the truth that he himself always remains "on the way." Though he performs the most sacred of actions, he remains a sinner in need of the grace and mercy that he mediates. He is himself always an "earthen vessel." In this way, the priest is always challenged (as the ordination rite expresses in many places) to live up to what he has been called to be.

The necessity of embracing his sacred mission and, at the very same time, always acknowledging his complete humanity is entirely in keeping with the Catholic sacramental sensibility—God makes himself present in the midst of the ordinary. The God who makes himself present in ordinary bread and wine, in the ordinary actions of eating and drinking, makes himself present, too, in the all-too-human life and action of a priest. This tension can serve as a challenge to the priest to thank God for calling one like himself, to give his ministry to God—who must bring any of the priest's efforts to completion—and to strive even more to live a life worthy of the sacred functions he has been called to carry out. Further, as we shall see, the very nature of the priest's ministry will challenge him to remember that his most sacred ministry is lived out most authentically in humble service.

A Life Truly Transformed

The rite of ordination of the priest does not simply suggest that a man has now received new functions in the Church; rather, it manifests a man whose life has been changed and transformed. Traditionally, it has been said that, through ordination, the priest is marked with a special "priestly character": he has undergone an "ontological change," a change at the level of his very being. Certainly, the ordination rite suggests that the ordinand's life is transformed through the action of the rite.

One of the most striking moments in the ordination is the prostration of the candidate on the floor of the Church during the singing of the Litany of the Saints. This is a posture of awe and wonder in the presence of the Holy, of complete self-giving and total surrender to a reality and to a call that transcends one's ability to stand and reason. This action is followed by a laying on of hands in a powerfully mysterious silence and a prayer that invokes the history of sacred ministry among the People of God. Rising to receive new vesture and welcome into the presbyteral brotherhood to which he now belongs, the new priest is now clearly something and someone that he was not. He has a new identity, a new focused purpose to his life, a new being.

In fact, priesthood is first a matter of *being* before it is a matter of *doing*. It is a matter of who we *are* before it is a matter of the *functions* we perform, no matter how sacred those functions may be. In the rite of ordination, through the action of the Spirit of God, a man has become a representative of Christ; he is to be Christ's presence through his life and ministry; he is empowered to act in Christ's name and in his person. Not just for a time, but for a lifetime.

Before Pope Pius XII made clear in 1947 that the laying on of hands is the "matter" of the sacrament, some theologians focused particular attention on the handing over of the paten and chalice to the ordinand. Reception of these principal vessels of his service at the altar highlighted the priest's sacred, cultic function. Pope Pius and the later post-conciliar reform of the ordination rite, however, make clear that the laying on of hands is the central act of ordination, that ordination is a matter of consecrating a whole person for a sacred mission rather than principally handing on a power to exercise a sacred function.

Priest, Prophet and King

Much of the doctrinal nature of the priesthood is revealed by a little reflection on the rite of ordination in light of papal and conciliar teachings on the priesthood. At the same time, the words and actions of the rite manifest both a greater specificity about the nature and functions of a priest as well as greater breadth of vision of the essential relationship of priests with bishops, with brother priests, and with the People of God.

Both the homily in the rite of ordination as well as the questions addressed to the candidate during the rite's examination provide a greater specificity to the meaning of the office which the ordinand is about to receive. By ordination, the priest will share in the threefold mission of Christ as Priest, Prophet and King: "He is to serve Christ the Teacher, Priest, and Shepherd in his ministry..." (Homily, paragraph 3). "By consecration he will be made a true priest of the New Testament, to preach the Gospel, sustain God's people, and celebrate the liturgy, above all, the Lord's sacrifice" (Homily, paragraph 4). In the three chapters which follow, we will reflect on each of the three aspects of priestly ministry as these are manifest in the rite of ordination.

Two

Priest as Preacher and Teacher

Homily, paragraphs 5 and 6:

"My son, you are now to be advanced to the order of the presbyterate. You must apply your energies to the duty of teaching in the name of Christ, the chief Teacher. Share with all mankind the word of God you have received with joy. Meditate on the law of God, believe what you read, teach what you believe, and put into practice what you teach.

"Let the doctrine you teach be true nourishment for the people of God. Let the example of your life attract the followers of Christ, so that by word and action you may build up the house which is God's Church."

Examination, question 3:

"Are you resolved to exercise the ministry of the word worthily and wisely, preaching the Gospel and explaining the Catholic faith?"

Prayer of Consecration:

"May he be faithful in working with the order of bishops, so that the words of the Gospel may reach the ends of the earth...."

* * *

The Second Vatican Council's *Decree on the Ministry and Life of Priests (Presbyterorum Ordinis)* states that "it is the first task of priests as co-workers of the bishops to preach the Gospel to all men" (PO 4). Pope John Paul II reiterates this teaching in his reflection on priestly formation, *I Will Give You Shepherds*

(*Pastores Dabo Vobis 26*): "The priest is first of all a *minister of the Word of God.*" Although he is ordained to continue Christ's threefold mission as prophet, priest and shepherd (LG 28: "...to preach the Gospel and shepherd the faithful as well as to celebrate divine worship as true priests of the New Testament"), the task of proclaiming, preaching and teaching the Word of God is fundamental to the life and ministry of the priest.

The centrality of preaching the Gospel in the ministry of the priest is, of course, consistent with the teaching of the Council about the ministry of bishops. *Lumen Gentium* (25) begins its reflection on the episcopal office by saying that preaching is the pre-eminent task of bishops. Among important episcopal duties, preaching has "pride of place." Only then, in the following sections (LG 26-27), does the conciliar document go on to reflect on the sacramental and pastoral leadership of bishops.

Preacher, Prophet, Evangelizer, Teacher

The priest's ministry of the Word is pre-eminently focused on the preaching ministry. The priest is a servant of the Word of God. He is not the master of the Word, nor is it his personal or sole possession (PDV 26). But it is his task to break open the Word that has been entrusted to the entire community in order to shed its light on their daily lives. It is not his own wisdom nor his own best judgment that the priest seeks to convey in his preaching. Rather, to the best of his ability, he strives to discern the message of God revealed in the Scripture for this particular community of disciples at this particular moment in its history.

The preaching task is therefore aptly described as a prophetic ministry. The priest continues the prophetic mission of Christ —"prophetic" not in the sense of forecasting the future but rather in the biblical sense of speaking on behalf of God. As the Council teaches, Christ himself speaks when the Scriptures are read in the Church (SC 7); and through his preaching, the priest strives to translate the Word of God for the lives of the People of God. The priest, as the minister of the Word, is the human voice of God. Certainly, at best, he is a frail and imperfect echo of God's voice; but by ordination, the priest is specially configured to Christ the Teacher and empowered by the Holy Spirit for just this prophetic task.

The pre-eminence of the preaching task means that the priest's ministry always has the character of evangelizing. The priest's entire life and ministry is aimed at speaking the Good News. This is apparent in the ordination rite's Prayer of Consecration: "May he be faithful in working with the order of bishops, so that the words of the Gospel may reach the ends of the earth…." In word and in action, especially in the act of preaching itself but more broadly as well, the priest is fundamentally an evangelizer.

Flowing from the ministry of the Word are also the broader tasks of teaching and catechizing. The priest is ordained to teach in the person and in the name of Christ the Teacher. As a co-worker with his own bishop, who is the first teacher of the local Church and with the order of bishops, the priest seeks to pass on the wisdom and the tradition of the Church—in its doctrine, in its history, in the lives of its saints, in its theology and in its liturgy—for the ongoing faith and life of the People of God.

"Worthily and Wisely"

But if the priest is pre-eminently a minister of the Word, a proclaimer and preacher of the Word, then he must take that duty seriously. And so, in the rite, the bishop asks the candidate for ordination: "Are you resolved to exercise the ministry of the word *worthily and wisely*, preaching the Gospel and explaining the Catholic faith?" [emphasis added]. Obviously, the candidate is asked to respond "I am" not only to the question of his resolve to undertake the ministry but also to do so "worthily and wisely."

I believe that the importance of the preaching task makes clear that preparation for preaching must be both serious and a real priority. Certainly, many priests are extremely busy attending to the many and varied ministerial tasks in their parishes. But if preaching is the "first task" of priests, if the priest is "first of all a minister of the Word of God," and if it is truly the Word of God and not merely some human word that is to be preached, then how can it be that so many other tasks seem to take up all of our time, leaving precious little time for more than a cursory preparation for Sunday preaching? In light of the conciliar and papal teaching on the fundamental importance of preaching—and in light of the solemn commitment to exercise this ministry "worthily and wisely"— how could a priest really justify letting everything else take up all of the time that could and should be dedicated to the preparation of a solid Sunday homily?

Some priests have natural gifts for speaking and for preaching. Other priests may have specialized training in preaching or in biblical studies. Many of us simply have to do the best that we can with whatever natural gifts and training we have. But the point is that we have to do our best. Surely the Word of God deserves it. Surely our priestly identity requires it. And this is what we promised, on the day of our ordination.

In the course of travels over the years, I have heard many bad homilies. I have given my own share of them. Sometimes, in preparation of a homily, one can sincerely and diligently study, pray and reflect, and yet the homily never seems to "come together" in a way that truly seems adequate. One of my colleagues says, quite correctly I think, that "sometimes you just have to preach the bad ones"—recognizing and trusting that God has the power to touch the hearers' lives well beyond the vessel of our words. In fact, most priests probably share the experience of having someone approach them after what the priest considers to have been a "bad homily" with the purpose of thanking the priest for the "wonderful homily" that touched his or her life in some profound way.

But there are some bad homilies that, it seems to me, are almost an affront to the Word of God—not because the priest wasn't blessed with natural gifts for preaching or because a particular image in the homily didn't work. I mean, rather, those homilies that seem to lack any serious preparation in the form of prayer, reflection, study or simple organization of one's thoughts. Obviously, extraordinary circumstances occur in all of our lives—an unexpected but important event, for example, suddenly requires our attention during the time that we had laid aside for serious homily preparation (in which case, a homily should probably be brief and to the point). But a habit of failing to take the time (or to *make* the time!) to prepare a good homily is, it seems to me, an insult to the Word of God. It cheats the People of God of the nourishment they need and deserve; it reneges on the promise made on one's ordination day to exercise the ministry of the Word "worthily and wisely." Walter Burghardt has said, quite aptly: "I do not minimize divine inspiration. I simply suggest that it is rarely allotted to the lazy."

Of course, preparation for the ministry of preaching is even more basic (and more challenging) than the preparation of individual homilies from week to week. In fact, it requires becoming, as Pope John Paul has said (PDV 26), truly familiar with the Word of God: "He needs to approach the word with a docile and prayerful heart, so that it may deeply penetrate his thoughts and feelings and bring about a new outlook in him—'the mind of Christ'...(1 Cor. 2:16)."

Through our own regular, prayerful encounter with the Scriptures—in the daily Eucharist, in the Liturgy of the Hours, in our private prayer—the Bible truly should become *our* personal book. We should become familiar with it, like an old friend. We should be able, more and more, to hear the voice of the Lord speaking to us in the Word.

The traditional monastic method of *lectio divina* is precisely a tool for this growing familiarity. *Lectio divina*, more than mere "spiritual reading," involves a deep, multilayered encounter with the Word of God. The scriptural text is read over, slowly and reflectively (*lectio*). Time is taken for reflection on its meaning for one's own life, perhaps aided by reference to a tool such as contemporary biblical commentary (*meditatio*). The person responds in a prayer from his own heart, praising God or asking for assistance or interceding for another (*oratio*). Finally, time is taken to sit in quiet, perhaps slowly repeating a phrase or a word from the text, waiting on a word of God spoken to the depths of one's heart (*contemplatio*). The daily practice of *lectio divina* over a long period of life brings a depth of familiarity with the Scriptures that can serve as fertile ground for preaching.

In the end, only a developing life of faith allows the priest to continue to keep his preaching fresh and new. Some texts— especially the very familiar ones—can be hard to preach. After a few years in a parish, the priest can begin to fear that he has exhausted ideas for his homilies, particularly, for example, in the long string of Johannine passages in the Sundays after Easter. Sometimes we must preach homilies that seem dry or all too familiar, trusting that God has a word yet to speak to this congregation through the best effort we have been able to make. My point here is simply that a regular life of prayer, fidelity to ongoing growth in the life of faith and a habit of daily encounter with the Scriptures, enriches our every encounter with biblical texts, even the most familiar.

But even a growing familiarity with the Scriptures is not sufficient preparation for preaching. We have a duty not only to become familiar with the Word of God, we have a duty to become increasingly *conformed* to the Word of God. As the ordination homily says so powerfully: "Meditate on the law of God, believe what you read, teach what you believe, and put into practice what you teach…. Let the example of your life attract the followers of Christ, so that by word and action you may build up the house which is God's Church."

In an important way, of course, our lives are slowly conformed to the Word by our regular meditation on the Word of God as it forms our vision, our identity, our priorities. This is so for every Christian. But the challenge of conforming our lives to the Gospel is issued even more urgently to priests who are told, in effect, to "practice what you preach."

How we live our lives as priests—how we interact with people on a daily basis, how we treat other people in our daily encounters, the apparent priorities of our own lives revealed in what takes up our time—all of these are an important aspect of our ministry of preaching and teaching. For better or worse, they give testimony to the People of God. Again, to promise that we are resolved to exercise the ministry of the Word "worthily and wisely" is a challenge to teach through our actions in a way increasingly consistent with the Word that we preach. Certainly, at the very minimum, our lives must not be a hindrance to the preaching of the Good News so, when people look at us, the message they see won't run contrary to what our words profess or make the Gospel seem lacking in credibility.

Preacher and Shepherd

Of course, our preaching and teaching task as priests is closely linked to carrying out the other two aspects of our share in Christ's ministry: pastoring and sanctifying. All three are, after all, merely different aspects of one mission.

Good teachers, of course, know their material well, and they love what they teach and they love teaching it. But good teachers also love their students. To exercise the ministry of the

Word "worthily and wisely," we must also be good shepherds
of the People of God—teaching them precisely *because*
we want to guide them, pastor them, lead them. And in our
shepherding, we must truly love them; otherwise our preaching
can become patronizing, moralizing, talking down to them, or
just plain dry and disconnected from their real lives. In fact, it
seems that people are willing to hear hard and challenging
things from priests whom they know truly love them.

The Committee on Priestly Life and Ministry of the
National Conference of Catholic Bishops makes clear in its
1982 document on preaching, *Fulfilled in Your Hearing: The
Homily in the Sunday Assembly*, that effective preaching requires
being familiar not only with the Word but also with the lives of
the people for whom that Word is spoken. Love, in fact, is a
way of knowing—in many ways, a deeper way of knowing. As
preachers and teachers, we must know *about* God, *about* the
Scriptures, *about* methods of preaching. But we must also
have a knowledge empowered by love for God, love for the
Scriptures and love for the wonderful task of preaching. At
the same time, we must not only know about the people to
whom we minister, we must know them with the deeper
knowledge of love, a shepherd's love for his flock. Love,
then, can empower and enliven our preaching.

It is certainly true, in fact, that many a parish community
is willing to overlook bad preaching because they recognize
that their priests love them. (The People of God are often
quite patient!) And such pastoral love is most surely to be
commended. Yet how much more effective would the priests be
if they showed their love through good preaching! How much

more effective our pastoral love would be if the deep and loving knowledge that we have of our people could help us to speak God's Word to the actual situations of their lives, as his love has revealed it to the priest himself.

The importance of knowing the people deeply and truly is vitally important for effective preaching. Interestingly, the Bishops' document on preaching, *Fulfilled in Your Hearing* (p. 29), defines the homily as a "scriptural interpretation of human existence." Perhaps we might rather have expected to be told that a homily is an interpretation *of the Scriptures.* In fact, in the end, preaching is meant to be not so much an interpretation of the Scriptures as much as it is an interpretation of the hearers' lives in light of the Word of God—God's Word "breaking open" the meaning of their lives. How important it is, then, for the preacher to know both the Word of God and this congregation of the People of God!

Preacher and Priest

The proclamation of the Word culminates, reaches its perfection, in the celebration of the Eucharist. The Eucharist, says the Council (PO 5), is "the source and summit of all preaching of the Gospel." And so, although preaching is his first task, his preaching, like every other aspect of his ministry, points to the Eucharist: "But the other sacraments, and indeed all ecclesiastical ministries and works of the apostolate are bound up with the Eucharist and are directed towards it" (PO 5).

In the liturgy, the priest proclaims the Word of God, which is the living reminder of God's saving deeds throughout history.

This proclamation leads naturally to the wonderful prayer of grateful remembering in which, together with the sacramental actions, Christ makes himself present, offering himself to us again and inviting us to offer our lives to God through him in grateful response. The proclamation and preaching of the Word is therefore directed precisely to our self-offering together with that of Christ in the Eucharistic action. In the Eucharist, Christ is present in the priest, in the baptized assembled, in the Word proclaimed, and in the Eucharistic species and actions. Together, they form a whole.

It is no accident, then, that the general expectation is that the one who presides at the Eucharist is also the one who preaches (FIYH, 2), since the Liturgy of the Word and the Liturgy of the Eucharist form "one single act of worship" (SC 56). Obviously, for sound pastoral reasons, this ideal is not always realized (the presence of deacons or visiting missionary priests, etc.), but it is nonetheless clear that the proclamation and preaching of the Word points to its fulfillment in the Eucharist. The priest's role as minister of the Word points to the role of both priest and shepherd.

Preaching and Conversion

The Council (PO 4) urges priests to take up the task of preaching as an "urgent invitation…to conversion and holiness." The encounter with the Word of God is always a challenge to accept the Good News: "Repent and believe the Good News!" (Mk 1:15). But it is a challenge that we issue not only to our hearers but which we implicitly accept for ourselves in the act of proclaiming and preaching. Each time that we, as priests, proclaim and preach the Word of God, we accept the challenge to take up the invitation given to *us* to conversion and holiness.

"Meditate on the law of God, believe what you read, teach what you believe, and put into practice what you teach." Because we are privileged to read, to proclaim, to hear the Word of God every day as its ministers—and because we have, so often, the challenge of conveying it to others—priests receive an ever-renewed challenge to take the Word to heart and to allow it to transform our lives. In the same way, because we preside so often at the Eucharist in which the People of God offer their "spiritual sacrifice," united with that of Christ, we experience a daily renewal of the invitation to surrender our own lives through the embrace of the Cross. And, because we are shepherds in the name and person of Jesus, we learn more and more to "serve and not to be served."

The rite of ordination, in word and action, manifests the Church's understanding of the nature of the priesthood and the priest's distinctive functions within the Church. But more, the rite manifests the challenge to priests to live the reality, the commitments and the identity we accepted on the day of our ordination. It is by faithfully being what we are called to be and doing what we are called to do that we priests will live our own ongoing conversion and attain holiness. As *Presbyterorum Ordinis* (13) says in a section titled "The Exercise of the Threefold Priestly Function both Demands and Fosters

Holiness": "Priests will acquire holiness in their own distinctive way by exercising their functions sincerely and tirelessly in the Spirit of Christ."

Three

The Priest in a Priestly Office

Homily, paragraph 2:

"It is true that God has made his entire people a royal priesthood in Christ. But our High Priest, Jesus Christ, also chose some of his followers to carry out publicly in the Church a priestly ministry in his name on behalf of mankind."

Homily, paragraphs 7 and 8:

"In the same way you must carry out your mission of sanctifying in the power of Christ. Your ministry will perfect the spiritual sacrifice of the faithful by uniting it to Christ's sacrifice, the sacrifice which is offered sacramentally through your hands. Know what you are doing and imitate the mystery you celebrate. In the memorial of the Lord's death and resurrection, make every effort to die to sin and to walk in the new life of Christ.

"When you baptize, you will bring men and women into the people of God. In the sacrament of penance, you will forgive sins in the name of Christ and the Church. With holy oil you will relieve and console the sick. You will celebrate the liturgy and offer thanks and praise to God throughout the day, praying not only for the people of God but for the whole world. Remember that you are chosen from among God's people and appointed to act for them in relation to God. Do your part in the work of Christ the Priest with genuine joy and love, and attend to the concerns of Christ before your own."

Examination, question 2:

"Are you resolved to celebrate the mysteries of Christ faithfully and religiously as the Church has handed them down to us for the glory of God and the sanctification of Christ's people?"

Anointing of Hands:

"The Father anointed our Lord Jesus Christ through the power of the Holy Spirit. May Jesus preserve you to sanctify the Christian people and to offer sacrifice to God."

* * *

The ordination homily begins: "It is true that God has made his entire people a royal priesthood in Christ. But our High Priest, Jesus Christ, also chose some of his followers to carry out publicly in the Church a priestly ministry in his name on behalf of mankind." By virtue of their baptism, all Christians share in the priesthood of Jesus Christ, a "common priesthood of all believers," as the Second Vatican Council calls it (LG 10). Every Christian participates in the priesthood of Christ by which the Son offers himself to the Father.

As a Christian, the priest shares in this common priesthood; but, by ordination, he shares in a unique way in the priesthood of Christ. The priesthood of the ordained, or the "ministerial priesthood," says the Council, is "essentially different" from the common priesthood. The two, however, are "ordered to one another." They have to be understood in relation to one another. In fact, says the Council, the priesthood of the ordained is meant to serve the priesthood of all believers.

What does the word *priesthood* mean when spoken of Jesus, of all the baptized, and of the ordained minister of the Catholic Church? [Although I have written at greater length about this topic in an earlier book, *In Persona Christi: Reflections on Priestly Identity and Holiness*, it is important to see how the ordination rite reveals the distinctive priestly office of the ordained in relationship to both the priesthood of Christ and the priesthood of all Christians.]

Participating in the Priesthood of Jesus

Jesus Christ is a Priest in his self-offering to the Father, most especially through his sacrifice on the Cross—in which he was both priest (offering the sacrifice) and the victim (the lamb of sacrifice). We see the priestly mission of Jesus most explicitly discussed in the Letter to the Hebrews. His self-offering on the Cross was the all-sufficient sacrifice that brought salvation to all. After Jesus, there is no need for any further sacrifice—no further need for a priesthood separate from his own. Any authentic priesthood, then, shares in *his* priesthood or it is simply no priesthood at all.

The followers of Jesus share in his priesthood by offering their own lives to the Father, in and through Christ and after his example. They do so by giving themselves in generous acts of love for others, by forgetting self in love for others, in selfless service of others. They do so, too, by "letting go" in trust—in the face of life's disappointments, tragedies, pains and struggles —as Jesus did upon the Cross. Thus, the Council speaks of the "spiritual sacrifice" offered by all of those who share in the priesthood of Christ (PO 2). All Christians realize their share in Christ's priesthood to the degree that they are able to surrender their lives in prayer and worship, in trust and in selfless action. The priesthood of all believers reaches its greatest fulfillment in this life in the Eucharist, in which their self-giving joins with that of Christ.

The ordained priest shares in this common priesthood and, like his brothers and sisters, he must offer his life in service, in loving and in trust. This is his "spiritual sacrifice" as a believer. But more, as an ordained priest, his distinctive priesthood is meant to serve, to form, to empower the self-giving of his brothers and sisters. By helping his people to see that all good gifts, all joy, all success come from God, he empowers them to offer gratefully these gifts back to God in service of others. By standing with his brothers and sisters in time of tragedy, loss, pain, illness and death, he strives to manifest that God stands with them—that God is worthy of their trust, that they must surrender to God in trust even in the face of these sufferings that are beyond their control. The ordained priest, then, helps the baptized to offer their "spiritual sacrifice" in the ordinary "stuff" of their lives—in joy and in sorrow, in success and in failure.

But his priestly service of the People of God is manifest most perfectly at the Eucharist, in which the People of God share in Christ's priestly action in a privileged way. As the ordination homily says: "Your ministry will perfect the spiritual sacrifice of the faithful by uniting it to Christ's sacrifice, the sacrifice which is offered sacramentally through your hands." The Second Vatican Council says: "However, it is in the eucharistic cult or in the eucharistic assembly of the faithful (*synaxis*) that they exercise in a supreme degree their sacred functions; there, acting in the person of Christ and proclaiming his mystery, they unite the votive offerings of the faithful to the sacrifice of Christ their head..." (LG 28).

Less explicitly but more powerfully, in the ordination rite, the distinctive priestly service of the ordained is manifest in the Presentation of the Gifts. Here the bishop urges the priest to accept the gifts to be offered at the Eucharist and then refers these gifts and the priest himself to the mystery of the Cross: "Accept from the holy people of God the gifts to be offered to him. Know what you are doing, and imitate the mystery you celebrate: model your life on the mystery of the Lord's cross." The People of God give to the newly ordained priest the gifts of bread and wine, which symbolize their own self-giving in union with the self-giving of Christ. Precisely in the bread broken and wine poured out—consumed for the life of the world—Christ, through the action of the ordained priest, will become present and will identify himself both with the people who offer their lives and with the priest who acts in his name as priest.

The ordained priest is never more clearly a priest, therefore, than when he presides at the Eucharist, gathering together the gifts of God's people to be united with the self-giving of Jesus. "The ministry of priests is directed to this and finds its consummation in it," says the Council (PO 2). Presiding at the Eucharist is by no means his entire ministry, but it reveals the shape and purpose of his priestly ministry in a special way.

A Mission of Sanctifying

The rite of ordination makes clear that the priestly office of the ordained is connected with the work of "sanctifying," of "making holy." The priest "blesses," "consecrates," "makes holy." As the ordination homily says: "In the same way you must carry out your mission of sanctifying in the power of Christ." In the rite's examination, the candidate is asked: "Are you resolved to celebrate the mysteries of Christ faithfully and religiously as the Church has handed them down to us for the glory of God and the sanctification of Christ's people?" As the bishop anoints the hands of the newly ordained priest, he says: "The Father anointed our Lord Jesus Christ through the power of the Holy Spirit. May Jesus preserve you to sanctify the Christian people and to offer sacrifice to God."

"Holiness," of course, is an attribute of God. God is holy in his transcendence, in his being "beyond" created existence, in being "other" than we are. A person, an action or an object is "holy" or "sacred" to the degree that each becomes like God, is "taken up into the life of God," or is made by God to be a mediation of his presence. Again, we see the Catholic sacramental principle: God in Christ makes himself present in the ordinary.

The ordained priest is set apart as a priest for sanctifying, making holy. This means he reveals God's presence in ordinary persons and actions and events (which is often what preaching involves), makes Christ present in sacramental actions, draws the "spiritual sacrifice" of ordinary men and women together into the sacrifice of Christ. And, of course, the priest himself is thereby challenged to become himself, more and more, a witness to the sacred, to the divine, to holiness—by drawing ever closer to God himself, by mediating God's presence ever more consistently, by developing that relationship with Christ that allowed St. Paul to say, "I live now, not I, but Christ lives in me" (Gal. 2:20).

In addition to the central place of the Eucharist in the priest's ministry, the ordination homily points also, more broadly, to the importance of the distinctive prayer of priests: "You will celebrate the liturgy and offer thanks and praise to God throughout the day, praying not only for the people of God but for the whole world." This is consistent with the teaching of the Council: "By the Office [Liturgy of the Hours] they pray to God in the name of the Church for the whole people entrusted to them and in fact for the whole world" (PO 5). Daily praying of the Liturgy of the Hours reveals that the priest is a priest in his prayer for the Church and for the world as well as in day-to-day ministry. He seeks to sanctify the world by bringing it daily into his own prayer and into the prayer of the Church.

Sanctifying the Priest's Own Life

To be a priest, then—continuing the mission of Jesus Christ, the One True High Priest—challenges the ordained in many ways in his own personal living. He is challenged to offer his own "spiritual sacrifice" more faithfully, surrendering his own life ever more fully in service, in trust, and love in the daily events and encounters of his life and ministry. He is challenged to be an authentic witness of this "spiritual sacrifice" for the People of God, since by ordination his entire life is dedicated to serving the people's priestly self-offering together with that of Christ. He is challenged to truly devote himself completely to a priestly ministry through which his brothers and sisters are enabled, empowered, formed to surrender their own lives to God, more and more.

Four

Priest as Shepherd

Homily, paragraph 9:

"Finally, conscious of sharing in the work of Christ, the Head and Shepherd of the Church, and united with the bishop and subject to him, seek to bring the faithful together into a unified family and to lead them effectively, through Christ and in the Holy Spirit, to God the Father. Always remember the example of the Good Shepherd who came not to be served but to serve, and to seek out and rescue those who were lost."

Examination, question 1:

"Are you resolved, with the help of the Holy Spirit, to discharge without fail the office of priesthood in the presbyteral order as a conscientious fellow worker with the bishops in caring for the Lord's flock?"

Prayer of Consecration:

"May he be faithful in working with the order of bishops, so that...the family of nations, made one in Christ, may become God's one, holy people."

* * *

The priest, as a shepherd, has a leadership role among the People of God. The priest shares in the "kingly" mission of Christ—the mission of "ruling"—as the older terms have expressed it. The primary theme of my earlier book on the priesthood is that the priest acts *in persona Christi capitis* (in the person of Christ as Head of the Church). Being a priest means to be a leader in the local community—a responsibility from which we ought not to shrink in this age and culture of egalitarianism.

Certainly, every organization needs effective leadership. And the ordination homily urges the priest to be an effective leader: "…seek to bring the faithful together into a unified family and to lead them effectively, through Christ and in the Holy Spirit, to God the Father."

But the priest is not a CEO. He is a *shepherd*-leader, a *pastoral* leader. His leadership is shaped, characterized and molded by a love for the people. And his leadership is aimed at leading the People of God, not to some earthly institutional goal but to God. The ordination homily states: "Finally, conscious of sharing in the work of Christ, the Head and Shepherd of the Church, and united with the bishop and subject to him, seek to bring the faithful together into a unified family and to lead them effectively, through Christ and in the Holy Spirit, to God the Father."

The priest exercises leadership in concrete and mundane earthly projects for the sake of the parish, but all of his leadership is aimed, ultimately, at bringing his people together into deeper communion with the Father. As the homily says, he seeks to lead his people "through Christ and in the Holy Spirit, to God the Father." Or, as the Second Vatican Council says (LG 28): "Exercising within the limits of the authority which is theirs, the office of Christ, the Shepherd and Head, they assemble the family of God in a brotherhood fired with a single ideal, and through Christ in the Spirit they lead it to God the Father."

It is important to note that the priest's task of leading people to God is also the task of bringing people *together*, gathering them together into one flock, one family of God, along the way. And so, the prayer of consecration says: "May he be faithful in working with the order of bishops, so that…the family of nations, made one in Christ, may become God's one, holy people." In short, it is clear that the priest as shepherd is called to form, build up and strengthen the Christian *community*, the fellowship of the pilgrim People of God on the way to God through Christ and in the Holy Spirit.

The priest's pastoral leadership is a multilayered reality. He gathers the people and he strives to lead them forward. It is no accident, it seems to me, that the Prayer of Consecration offers explicit mention of Moses as a pastoral leader of the people of Israel, while many of the great leaders of the Old Testament remain unnamed. Moses "ruled" the people, as the rite says. He exercised leadership, leading the people together to the Promised Land. Certainly not explicit in the rite, but interesting in its possible implications for the pastoral leadership of priests, is the fact that the Church Fathers (most notably, Gregory of Nyssa in his *Life of Moses*) saw Moses as one of the first great mystics of our tradition.

Moses met God in the burning bush upon "holy ground"; he went up the mountain to speak directly to God; he entered the divine cloud that came down upon the tent of meeting. Moses, then, invoked by the prayer of consecration, was both a shepherd-leader and a mystic who spoke for God. He "mediated" between the divine and the human, based on a deep personal encounter with God, leading the people to the

Promised Land. In short, the figure of Moses offers an interesting and potentially powerful metaphor for priestly leadership.

The priest is, of course, a shepherd who cares for the flock of another. His pastoring flows from the call of the True Shepherd. Fundamentally, the flock is Christ's flock. The direction is the direction set by Christ. Priests have the responsibility of shepherding well, but we have the freedom to see that the task is really Christ's task, in which we participate by his grace. We can be shepherds who care while, at the same time, we can also be shepherds who can "let go" and leave those things which are beyond our power to the True Shepherd.

The Vision of a Leader

Much of the contemporary literature on leadership suggests that a leader—as distinct from a manager—must be a person of vision. Leaders must be firmly grounded in the organization's mission even as they must have a wider vision of the direction in which the organization should move. They should be able to "dream" the organization's future, seeing new possibilities. And they should be able to hold out the vision for the people to see and follow.

I think this literature on leadership has a lot to offer priests as leaders in the Church. Priests must have a sense of vision for a parish—the direction in which we need to move, a sense of the priorities, a sense of where we are going. Yet the priest, as a shepherd-leader, must have a more basic vision, one born of faith, formed by love and empowered by hope. He must see the

People of God (even those he doesn't like or doesn't agree with) as brothers and sisters placed in his pastoral care. (This can be a real challenge for all priests because we are very human shepherds with our own likes, dislikes and personal preferences.)

The priest must see that his ministry is always a ministry of unity, of reconciliation, of bringing together. (And this too can be a real challenge because we often have our own strong opinions, convictions and plans.) But because he is a shepherd, the priest must always strive to be a "bridge-builder" (a *pontifex*). He must see the present struggles, conflicts, challenges, tasks, plans and projects in light of the ultimate goal of bringing the flock together in the divine life. And, in light of *that* vision and goal, many of the present events of life can be seen from a different perspective.

Who Came To Serve

By definition, the priest has a real leadership role in the Church community. Of course, the ordination rite reminds us of the Shepherd whom we represent: "Always remember the example of the Good Shepherd who came not to be served but to serve, and to seek out and rescue those who were lost." Yes, the priest is a leader, but it is a leadership characterized by self-giving. The priest is not like the hireling who works for pay, who runs at the first sign of danger to himself. He is a shepherd who is willing to lay down his life for the sheep (as we do every day in our ministry as priests).

Priestly leadership, then, is a shepherding that ought not to be marked by seeking after power, control or status. In fact, there is a certain paradox: leadership, yes, but a servant-leadership, leading through serving others. Yes, the Church is hierarchical, as the Second Vatican Council affirmed, but this does not mean the priest is meant to lord over the people. Servant-leadership involves a distinctive form of pastoral asceticism: "As rulers of the community they cultivate the form of asceticism suited to a pastor of souls, renouncing their own convenience, seeking not what is to their own advantage but what will benefit the many for salvation, always making further progress towards a more perfect fulfillment of their pastoral work..." (PO 13).

In fact, even to speak of the priest sharing in the mission of Jesus as "King" and his mission of "ruling" points to the same implication for the life and ministry of the priest. We see the paradoxical nature of the kingship of Christ—the kingship in which we, all the baptized, share—in celebrating the feast of Christ the King. We certainly celebrate Christ as triumphant King of the Universe—Lord of Lords and King of Kings—and we look forward to the day when the fullness of his Kingdom will be realized. But, we recall, too, that in his human existence, this was a king who knelt down to wash the feet of his disciples, whose earthly crown was a crown of thorns, whose earthly throne was the Cross upon which he gave his life for his people. To say, then, that we share in the "kingly" or "ruling" mission of Christ is also paradoxical because it implies our imitation of the service and sacrifice that Christ so willingly gave.

With the Love of a Shepherd

Pope John Paul II emphasizes that our lives and ministry as priests ought to be animated by, shaped by, empowered by "pastoral charity." The life and ministry of priests ought to be marked by the shepherd's love for his people. Certainly, every Christian life ought to be marked by charity, by love. But the priest's life ought to be shaped by his love (his self-giving, his self-offering) for the people he leads and serves. Through ordination, he has *become* a shepherd; the role of a pastor is who and what the priest is. The *Directory* (13) says: "Called to the act of supernatural love, absolutely gratuitous, the priest should love the Church as Christ has loved her, consecrating to her all of his energies and giving himself with pastoral charity in a continuous act of generosity."

I think that the notion of pastoral charity reveals, in a deeper way, the meaning of priestly celibacy. The challenge of giving oneself in love, for the married person, is lived, in the first instance, by the love shown toward spouse and family. But the distinctive challenge for giving oneself in love, for the celibate priest, is lived in a self-giving for the People of God, i.e., in laying down one's life for the flock. As a shepherd, one's attention, time and priorities are given to the flock entrusted to our care. Celibacy is at the service of a love for God and for the People of God; and, through a celibate life, the priest seeks a more wholehearted availability to the people whom he shepherds.

In fact, the life of pastoral charity is our path to our distinctive holiness as priests. The holiness of the priest is found precisely in ministry and not separate from it. In the life of the priest, prayer is meant to empower ministry and ministry is meant to be taken up into prayer. Neither ministry instead of prayer nor prayer instead of ministry, but a prayerful ministry and a ministerial prayer. The priest's path to holiness is realized in his daily self-giving in service and in trust and in love in the ordinary course of his ordinary ministry. The priest's path to holiness is manifest most especially, once again, at the Eucharist in which the pastor's love for the People of God is united with the love of the True Shepherd for the flock that is truly Christ's flock.

Five

A Co-worker with the Bishop

Homily, paragraph 2:

"Priests are co-workers of the order of bishops. They are joined to the bishops in the priestly office and are called to serve God's people."

Homily, paragraph 4:

"He is called to share in the priesthood of the bishops and to be molded into the likeness of Christ, the supreme and eternal Priest."

Homily, paragraph 9:

"Finally, conscious of sharing in the work of Christ, the Head and Shepherd of the Church, and united with the bishop and subject to him, seek to bring the faithful together...."

Promise of Obedience:

"Do you promise respect and obedience to me and my successors?"

Prayer of Consecration:

"Come to our help, Lord, holy Father, almighty and eternal God; you are the source of every honor and dignity, of all progress and stability. You watch over the growing family of man by your gift of wisdom and your pattern of order. When you had appointed high priests to rule your people, you chose other men next to them in rank and dignity to be with them and to help them in their task; and so there grew up the ranks of priests and the offices of levites, established by sacred rites.

"In the desert you extended the spirit of Moses to seventy wise men who helped him to rule the great company of his people. You shared among the sons of Aaron the fullness of their father's power, to provide worthy priests in sufficient number for the increasing rites of sacrifice and worship. With the same loving care you gave companions to your Son's apostles to help in teaching the faith: they preached the Gospel to the whole world.

Lord, grant also to us such fellow workers, for we are weak and our need is greater.

Almighty Father, grant to this servant of yours the dignity of the priesthood. Renew within him the Spirit of holiness. As a co-worker with the order of bishops may he be faithful to the ministry that he receives from you, Lord God, and be to others a model of right conduct.

May he be faithful in working with the order of bishops, so that the words of the Gospel may reach the ends of the earth, and the family of nations, made one in Christ, may become God's one, holy people."

* * *

In the last three chapters, we have been examining the nature of the priesthood as reflected in the rite of ordination. In particular, we have been looking at the priest as one who continues and shares in the threefold mission and ministry of Christ: as preacher/teacher, as priest, and as shepherd/leader. But to recognize the threefold ministry of the priest does not yet complete the understanding of the priesthood as reflected in the rite itself. In fact, the ordination rite clearly understands the priesthood in relationship to others. Certainly, as we have seen, the rite presupposes that the priest is in a special relationship with Christ himself; but the rite also understands the priesthood in its relation with the bishops, with other priests, and with the People of God. This view flows from the teaching of the Council in its *Decree on the Ministry and Life of Priests*. In the reflections which follow in these next three chapters, we will look successively at the priest in relationship to each of these three groups.

A Co-worker with the Bishop

Perhaps one of the clearest messages of the ordination rite is that the priest must be understood to be a co-worker with the bishop. In fact, the greater part of the consecratory prayer is an appeal by the bishop for co-workers like those whom God has called throughout salvation history to share in the work of leading the People of God. In the rite, the ordaining bishop concludes this first part of the Prayer of Consecration by asking: "Lord, grant also to us such fellow workers, for we are weak and our need is greater."

It must be said first of bishops that they participate in the ministerial priesthood of Jesus Christ. Priests then share in the priesthood of Jesus as co-workers with the bishop. It is the order of bishops that principally continues the mission of Jesus as Teacher, Priest and Shepherd; priests share with the bishops in the office of preaching and teaching the People of God, and it is under his bishop's pastoral leadership of the People of God that the priest exercises his own pastoral role. The practice of concelebration around the bishop, particularly at ordinations and at the Chrism Mass on Holy Thursday, symbolizes the unity of the priests with their bishop.

In the earliest stage of the development of the ministerial priesthood, "presbyters" were a sort of council of "elders" gathered around the bishop. Their principal purpose, as a group, was to advise the bishop. But, as the Church began to grow and local congregations developed, the presbyters began to preside at the Eucharist in these local congregations, as representatives of the bishop. Even today, the bishop's name is always mentioned in the Eucharistic Prayer throughout his diocese, symbolic of the relationship of every local community and its pastor with the diocese's chief pastor. In fact, during the Eucharist, the practice of breaking off a small piece of the consecrated host and placing it in the chalice of consecrated wine comes from the practice of the early Church in which a fraction from the bishop's Eucharistic Liturgy was brought to each of the communities in which his presbyters were presiding in his place.

Much later in the history, however, this original priority of the episcopal office was obscured. It came to be believed by many theologians that priesthood was primary, and bishops were a sort of "super-priest," that is, bishops were seen to be simply priests who had additional juridical or administrative power. One of the achievements of the Second Vatican Council was to restore the ancient understanding of the relationship of bishop and priest, an understanding reflected throughout the rite of ordination.

Through the Laying on of Hands

The essential action of the rite of ordination is the laying on of hands by the bishop, followed by the Prayer of Consecration. This is the ancient practice of the Church for setting apart bishops and presbyters, attested to in the New Testament. Through the laying on of hands by the bishop: (1) the bishop confirms that the priest's call is from Christ; (2) he unites the priest with the apostolic tradition; and (3) he connects the priest to the universal Church for the sake of mission.

(1) The call to the priesthood comes from Christ himself through the bishop who stands in the apostolic succession. In the ordination homily, the bishop says that, although all of the baptized share in a common priesthood, "our High Priest, Jesus Christ, also chose some of his followers to carry out publicly in the Church a priestly ministry in his name…." In the Prayer of Consecration, the bishop recalls that it was God who chose other men to assist the high priests of Israel; it was God who extended the spirit to the seventy wise men who helped Moses to rule; it was God who shared Aaron's power with his sons; it was God who gave companions to his Son's apostles; and, in the rite, the bishop asks that God will give him fellow workers as well.

The rite says the people give "consent" or "assent" to the election of the ordinand by the bishop, but the rite itself does not seem to support a contemporary notion that the community of believers calls forth members for a leadership ministry. In the prayer of consecration, the bishop says: "…may he be faithful to the ministry that he receives from you, Lord God…." In short, it seems simply to be assumed within the rite that Christ himself calls priests to represent him and to act in his name and in his person as Head and Shepherd of the people. Standing in the apostolic succession and acting in the person of Christ as Head and Shepherd of the Church, the bishop calls the candidates to Holy Orders.

(2) Further, standing within the apostolic succession, the bishop represents the long history and tradition of the Church. By the action of the laying on of hands, the priest is drawn into ("consecrated to") that tradition of pastoral leadership, teaching and sanctifying that extends back to the ministry of Jesus himself. It is in union with the bishop that the priest stands in union with the apostolic tradition and with the Gospel that is handed on by the Church; it is as a co-worker with the bishop that he carries on that task for the People of God in every new generation.

(3) The bishop is the source of unity within the local Church, and he is the symbol of the unity of the local Church with the universal Church. Together with his brother priests in a presbyteral fraternity, the newly ordained priest is joined through the bishop in the work of shepherding the diocese. His ministry is united with the mission of the universal Church and he shares in the task of striving to bring the family of nations into one in Christ as God's one, holy people.

The relationship of a priest to his bishop, therefore, must be understood not merely in juridic, legal or administrative terms but as a sacramental relationship. Every large organization has its administrative flow charts, its administrative structures, its policies and procedures. Certainly as a human (as well as a divine) institution, the Church has its own administrative structures; but the bond between the priest and his bishop is not principally an administrative connection of a middle manager with a top manager. The priest is connected to his bishop because his priesthood itself is sacramentally connected with the bishop's priesthood and with that of his brother priests. The laying on of hands during the rite of ordination symbolizes this deeper sacramental bond.

For the Sake of Mission

The relationship of bishop and priest is ultimately for *mission*; it is the service of that mission that gives shape and direction to their relationship. The Prayer of Consecration makes their common mission clear: "May he be faithful in working with the order of bishops, so that the words of the Gospel may reach the ends of the earth, and the family of nations, made one in Christ, may become God's one, holy people." As Pope John Paul II has taught emphatically: "consecration is for mission" (PDV 24).

Through ordination by the bishop, the priest commits himself completely to the mission of spreading the Good News to the ends of the earth and helping to gather all people together into God's holy people. He does so, by the very definition of his office, as a co-worker with the bishop. His priestly office is a participation in the bishop's office. A shepherd himself, he accepts the pastoral leadership of the diocese's chief shepherd. In the end, it is not his preferences, his priorities or his plans that are ultimately important to him. What is essential is the mission that he shares with his bishop and to which he has freely and completely dedicated his life and ministry. By ordination, the mission gives definition and direction to his entire life.

A Collaborative Relationship

The rite of ordination never speaks of the priest as a "servant" of the bishop, though it does say that the ministry of the priest, under obedience, is "subject" to the bishop for the care of the flock. In the ordination rite, the priest is referred to primarily as a "co-worker" or "fellow worker" of the bishops. They share together in the priestly office of Jesus, the one True High Priest. They share the mission of shepherding the People of God, "through Christ and in the Holy Spirit to God the Father." As the Congregation for the Clergy has said:

> With full respect for hierarchical subordination, the priest will promote a genuine rapport with his Bishop, indicated by sincere confidence, cordial friendship, and true effort towards consonance and convergence in ideals and programs. Nothing should take away from the intelligent capacity for personal initiative and pastoral enterprise. (*Directory* 24)

Recognizing that the priest is subject to the bishop, symbolized by his promise of obedience, it nonetheless seems clear that the ordination rite portrays the relationship of bishop and priest as a "collaboration" for the sake of the mission.

Certainly, the relationship of a priest to his bishop is a sacramental one, and therefore a very distinct type of relationship. At the same time, the very fact that the priestly office is by definition a collaborative one (as he is a "co-worker") suggests to me that contemporary discussion of collaboration among ordained and lay ministers, while respecting the distinctive identities and ministries involved, is in keeping with the nature of the priestly office. The priest is, by definition, a collaborator (principally and sacramentally with the bishop and his fellow priests) for the sake of mission. Perhaps it is not too much of a stretch to suggest that the priestly office is inherently collaborative with others as well, again for the sake of mission. This is even suggested when the Pope, in describing the shepherding and governing role of priests (PDV 26), says that it "also involves the ability to coordinate all the gifts and charisms which the Spirit inspires in the community, to discern them and to put them to good use for the upbuilding of the Church in constant union with the Bishops."

The Promise of Obedience

The promise of obedience made in the context of the rite is really a specification of the relationship of the priest with the bishop and of the priest's complete dedication of his life to mission. Obedience is not merely a matter of a legal arrangement, nor is it simply a practical matter of insuring the orderly administration of an organization. Seminarians (especially those who have come to the seminary after some time in the work force) sometimes speak at first about obedience as a matter of "following orders" or abiding "company policy," as they did in the workplace. If they could follow the orders of their managers and abide company directives in their previous work experience, then they see no reason to expect that they will have trouble promising obedience. At one level, their proven ability to follow orders and live within company directives is not a bad indication at all. However, the priest's promise of obedience really runs much deeper.

As we have seen, the priest's promise of obedience must be distinguished from the orderly administrative functioning of a secular organization. At the same time, the priest's promise of obedience must also be distinguished from the vow of obedience made by a monk to his religious superior. They are similar in their effect, but not the same in their basic purpose and therefore not in their scope.

The vow of obedience by a Benedictine monk is fundamentally a spiritual tool for rooting out self-will or, stated more positively, a commitment to develop a listening and docile spirit to the will of God as this is manifest in the command of one's superior. Presuming that every Christian life involves a surrender of one's self to God in trust and in love, the monk's vow of obedience is a tool for practicing and forming this surrender. Committing himself to accept even directives that he does not understand or with which he does not entirely agree can help form and strengthen in the monk the more basic spiritual surrender that is at the heart of the Christian life. Even in a day of dialogue, consultation and consensus-building, the fundamental value of a monastic vow of obedience remains.

Certainly, diocesan priests can and do grow in their own surrender to God through accepting the decisions of their bishops. Accepting an assignment that one does not particularly want can be an invitation and a challenge to let go of one's own control of life. The struggle to accept a decision in a spirit of obedience can be a powerful force to a deeper surrender in the priest's life and to a greater openness to the ways that God can work around, in spite of, or contrary to our own plans and expectations. On the other hand, the refusal of obedience *can* be a sign that the priest has put his own agenda ahead of the needs of the local Church, as discerned by the one charged with the care of the local Church. This is a matter of external conformity, but it is also a matter of spiritual openness.

While this personal challenge to obey can be valuable to the priest's own spiritual journey, priestly obedience is at the service of mission. Again, as the Prayer of Consecration says, in working with the bishop, the priest's ministry is directed to spreading the Gospel and promoting the unity of God's people. Just as "consecration is for mission" (in the words of the Pope), so, too, we can say that obedience is for mission. More specifically, obedience is for unity—for unity with the bishop who is chief shepherd of the local Church and successor of the apostles, for unity with one's fellow priests who share together in the common mission, and for accomplishing the unity of the People of God for whom he has been consecrated.

Priestly obedience is focused on the effectiveness of ministry, and importantly but only indirectly to the question of the priest's personal spiritual growth. In ordination, the priest gives his life over to the service of the People of God in the local Church, and his prostration during the rite of ordination gives powerful witness to this self-giving. Obedience represents his willingness to live up to that commitment. And the bishop, as the chief shepherd of the local Church and as the symbol of the unity of the Church, is given authority to decide what is in the best interests of the local Church. As Pope John Paul has said (PDV 28):

> The "submission" to those invested with ecclesial authority is in no way a kind of humiliation. It flows instead from the responsible freedom of the priest who accepts not only the demands of an organized and organic ecclesial life, but also that grace of discernment and responsibility in ecclesial decisions which was assured by Jesus to his Apostles and their successors, for the sake of faithfully safeguarding the mystery of the Church and serving the structure of the Christian community along its common path towards salvation.

No claim is made that the bishop, acting alone within his diocese, is infallible, omniscient or free from sin (which is all the more reason for the bishop to consult widely and to act collaboratively). The priest's obedience is not naive to the human factors in ecclesial decision-making (as he is not naive about his own leadership at the parish level). Yet the priest must recognize that a special charism gives a greater presumption to the decision of the bishop.

Obedience, therefore, is a reflection of the priest's own fundamental identity, his relationship with his bishop, and his freely chosen subordination of his own plans to the needs of the Church in fulfillment of its evangelizing and unifying mission. The priest's life and ministry are to be animated by pastoral charity, that is, by the shepherd's love in which the shepherd lays down his life for the sheep. He thinks of the needs of the people before his own desires and convenience.

More broadly, as Pope John Paul has said, priestly obedience must be understood in a communal way (PDV 28). The priest's promise of obedience exists within the context of the unity of the entire presbyterate with the bishop. It is not simply a matter of each individual priest's obedience to the bishop, but the relationship of the presbyterate with the bishop who is chief shepherd of the diocese and who therefore must coordinate the ministry of all of the priests in his diocese. In fact, one priest told me that he always challenges himself and his brother priests to "put themselves in the bishop's shoes." Surely to remember that the bishop has to take into consideration many different factors and needs for the sake of the entire diocese can make it easier to accept the sometimes difficult decisions that he must make.

An Attitude of Respectful Listening

The actual experience of living the promise of obedience will vary for different priests, at different points in their lives, in various dioceses, under different bishops. Of course, in many larger dioceses, priests may not often see their bishops personally. Probably, for most priests, it will (hopefully) be a rather rare occurrence to be confronted with the challenge to live his promise of obedience in the face of a decision with which he disagrees. In a world of collaboration and dialogue, at least a grudging agreement can often be attained about decisions. Certainly, while a bishop, on occasion, may feel it necessary to invoke a priest's promise of obedience as a sort of "last resort," surely this would be a final stage following upon some effort to reach a mutual agreement. Rare or not, however, the priest must be prepared to live out the promise he made on the day of his ordination; it is perhaps this spirit of readiness that reveals a deeper, more spiritual reality to which the promise of obedience points.

Obedience is really a matter of respectful listening, as its Latin root suggests. The priest, by ordination, is a man totally dedicated to carrying forward the mission of the Church. He is a man *of* the Church and a man *for* the Church. His very identity is thereafter connected with this reality. As a co-worker with his bishop and his fellow priests, he represents Christ in the pastoral care of the Church. As such, he is a man who listens for the voice of the Spirit as the Spirit directs the Church. Of course, the Spirit speaks in many places and in many ways, but the priest accepts the fact that those entrusted with the pastoral care of the Church have a special charism for leading and guiding the Church. It is for this reason that the priest should be especially attentive and open to the official teachings of the Pope and bishops, and he should be open to the directives of his bishop for the needs of the diocese for which he shares a real concern.

The promise of obedience, therefore, points to a more basic attitude of listening, of openness, of docility that should characterize the life of the priest. Ultimately, the priest listens attentively for the Spirit of God, but he promises a ready presumption that the Spirit will speak in the chief shepherd of the diocese who oversees the priest's own pastoral leadership.

Six

In the Presbyteral Order

Introduction:

"The priest concelebrates with the bishop in his ordination Mass. It is most appropriate for the bishop to admit other priests to the concelebration; in this case and on this day the newly ordained priest takes the first place ahead of the others who concelebrate."

Election by the Bishop:

"We rely on the help of the Lord God and our Savior Jesus Christ, and we choose this man, our brother, for priesthood in the presbyteral order."

Homily, paragraph 1:

"This man, your relative and friend, is now to be raised to the order of priests."

Homily, paragraph 3:

"Our brother has seriously considered this step and is now to be ordained to priesthood in the presbyteral order."

Homily, paragraph 5:

"My son, you are now to be advanced to the order of the presbyterate."

Examination, introduction:

"My son, before you proceed to the order of the presbyterate, declare before the people your intention to undertake this priestly office."

Examination, question 1:

"Are you resolved, with the help of the Holy Spirit, to discharge without fail the office of priesthood in the presbyteral order as a conscientious fellow worker with the bishops in caring for the Lord's flock?"

Laying on of Hands, instructions:

"Next all the priests present, wearing stoles, lay their hands upon the candidate in silence. After the laying on of hands, the priests remain on either side of the bishop until the prayer of consecration is completed."

Investiture with Stole and Chasuble, instructions:

"After the prayer of consecration, the bishop, wearing his miter, sits, and the newly ordained stands. The assisting priests return to their places, but one of them arranges the stole of the newly ordained as it is worn by priests and vests him in a chasuble."

Kiss of Peace, instruction:

"If circumstances permit, the priests present also give the kiss of peace to the newly ordained."

* * *

As seminary rector, I ask bishops what they believe needs to be emphasized in priestly formation today. One point that several bishops have mentioned to me over the last three years is that they think those preparing for priesthood today must have a stronger sense of their commitment to be an active participant in the life of the presbyterate of their diocese. These bishops report to me that some priests—especially some younger priests—don't seem very committed to attending traditional gatherings of priests: clergy days, Chrism Mass, the funerals of older priests, priest retreats within a diocese. And, at these gatherings, some younger priests seem to gather by themselves rather than try to get to know the older priests.

Some of this reticence of younger and older priests to mix with one another is, of course, simply generational. The very fact that the Council, in 1965, was urging older and younger priests to respect and collaborate with one another suggests that the problem is not new. Still, as these bishops have suggested, there is a deeper issue than a "generation gap" at stake here.

The Rite and the Presbyteral Fraternity

The rite of ordination makes the special and foundational relationship of the priest with other priests in his diocese extremely clear. Certainly there are ample explicit references to joining the Order of Presbyters throughout the homily, the examinations, the instructions and the prayers. But, even without the explicit words, the liturgical actions of the rite would make this fact abundantly clear.

The bishop is encouraged to allow concelebration at the ordination liturgy, resulting in the usual practice of having a large number of vested priests participating in the ordination rite itself. As the Congregation for the Clergy, in its *Directory for the Life and Ministry of Priests* (23), says of concelebration in general: "The Eucharistic concelebration itself...especially when presided by the Bishop and with the participation of the faithful, manifests well the unity of the priesthood of Christ in his ministers, as well as the unity of the sacrifice of the People of God. Moreover, it contributes to the consolidation of sacramental fraternity which exists among priests."

Further, the rite says that "all of the priests present, wearing stoles" (the sign of their office) should follow the bishop in the laying on of hands. The *Directory* (25) says of this practice: "The rite of imposition of hands by the Bishop and all of the priests present during the priestly Ordination has special significance and merit because it points to the equality of participation in the ministry, and to the fact that the priest cannot act by himself; he acts within the presbyterate becoming a brother of all who constitute it." The special bond of priestly fraternity, says the Council (PO 8), "is signified liturgically from ancient times by the fact that the priests present at an ordination are invited to impose hands, along with the ordaining bishop, on the chosen candidate, and when the priests concelebrate the sacred Eucharist in a spirit of harmony."

The rite calls for one of the assisting priests to help the newly ordained priest in the investiture with stole and chasuble. A more senior member of the presbyterate therefore helps the newly ordained priest take on the distinctive vesture that marks the presbyteral order in their liturgical functions. The practice in some dioceses of allowing the ordinand's parents or some other lay persons to vest the ordinand obscures this important symbol of the newly ordained priest incorporated into the presbyteral ranks.

In a similar way, the rite says that "if circumstances permit," the priests present should follow the bishop in giving the kiss of peace to the newly ordained. The members of the presbyteral order welcome their new brother into their fraternity. Many of the laity who participate in an ordination liturgy often report that watching the long line of priests lay hands on the ordinand and then give to him the sign of peace is one of the most moving parts of the ordination rite. Its symbolism is not lost on them.

All of these liturgical actions point to the special relationship of this newly ordained priest with the priests present. Whatever has happened to the ordinand in this rite, the rite makes clear that he has a special relationship both with the bishop and with these other priests.

In fact, the very term *ordination* refers to "joining" or "receiving" an "ordo"—an order, a distinct grouping. As *The Catechism of the Catholic Church* (#1537) explains, from the time of Roman antiquity, the word *ordo* referred to an established civil body, a distinct group, especially a governing body. The term was taken over into the early Church to refer especially to the episcopal, presbyteral and diaconal orders. Through this ordination, the candidate is received into the presbyteral order.

A "Radical Communitarian Form"

The priests of a diocese, around their bishop, form one presbyterate, sharing together in the ministry of Christ as Shepherd and Head of the Church. Pope John Paul II says that the priesthood has a "radical communitarian form" that must be "carried out as a collective work" (PDV 17). Together, bishop and priests are dedicated to one mission, especially in the local Church: evangelization and gathering people into the one People of God. Their ministry ought to take place with a spirit of mutual cooperation, support and assistance. The Council (LG 28) makes this bond and this shared task clear when it teaches: "In virtue of their sacred ordination and of their common mission all priests are united together by bonds of intimate brotherhood...."

In fact, Pope John Paul speaks of the presbyterate forming "a true family," a bond of fraternity that does not arise because of flesh and blood but because of the sacrament of Orders (PDV 17). The presbyterate is, the Pope says, a *mysterium*—a bond rooted in the sacrament of Orders—that in turn "takes up," "elevates" bonds of collaboration, friendship, and affection between and among priests. Each priest, in communion with his bishop and specially configured to Christ for their one shared mission, is therefore necessarily related to his brother priests.

Belonging to the Local Church

As part of a particular presbyterate, the priest is also part of a particular local Church. The term "incardination" expresses the legal, juridic bond of a priest with a particular diocese, but it points to a deeper relationship of the priest to the local Church (PDV 31, *Directory* 26). The presbyteral order is always focused on a particular diocese under the pastoral leadership of its bishop. In fact, the unity of the pastors of a diocese symbolizes

the unity of the parishes themselves under the pastoral care of
the diocese's chief shepherd.

The local Church, with its particular culture and history and
its particular people and priests, becomes the "place" in which
the priest exercises his ministry, offers his gifts and realizes his
own holiness. And so, the *Directory* (27) refers to the
presbyterate as the priest's "place of sanctification."

Support and Assistance

The grace of the priestly fraternity is realized practically in
the support and assistance, material and spiritual, that priests
offer to one another. As the Council says (PO 8):

> From this it follows that older priests should sincerely
> accept the younger ones as brothers and be a help to them
> in facing the first tasks and responsibilities of their ministry.
> They should make an effort also to understand their
> outlook even though it may be different from their own,
> and should give kindly encouragement to their projects.
> Young priests for their part are to respect the age and
> experience of their elders; they ought to consult with them
> on matters concerning the care of souls and willingly
> cooperate with them.
>
> Under the influence of the spirit of brotherhood priests
> should not forget hospitality and should cultivate kindness
> and the sharing of goods. They should be particularly
> concerned about those who are sick, about the afflicted, the
> overworked, the lonely, the exiled, the persecuted. They

should also be delighted to gather together for relaxation, remembering the words by which the Lord himself invited his weary apostles: "Come apart into a desert place and rest a little." (Mk. 6:31)

These words were issued by the Council in 1965. They remain relevant almost 35 years later. In 1965, many of today's middle-aged pastors were the seminarians and young priests who considered the older priests of the time to be conservative and out of touch with the times. And many of those older priests of the time considered the seminarians and younger priests of 1965 to be liberal iconoclasts. The Council urged priests of different ages to come together in mutual respect and support in the context of their fraternal relationship within the presbyterate.

The words of the Council issued in 1965 still speak in a valuable way to a different situation today, though almost the reversal of the pattern 35 years ago. Today many middle-aged pastors look at seminarians and younger priests and judge them to be conservative and even reactionary. Many seminarians and younger priests look at their middle-aged pastors and judge them to be liberal and "loose" about Church doctrine and practice. As they did some 35 years ago, the words of the Second Vatican Council urge priests of different generations and ecclesial viewpoints to recognize their presbyteral communion and to offer the respect and support that their brother priests need and deserve.

Times change. Each generation is different from the one that came before. Some of the projects and plans of the current generation will be put aside by the next generation. Each new generation will make its share of missteps. Yet, the Church is ultimately protected, guided and moved forward by the power of the Holy Spirit. Disagreement and even conflict can be a good thing; but those who trust in the working of the Spirit in human action—and sometimes *in spite* of human action—can keep disagreement from becoming disdain and conflict, from becoming warfare.

At a practical level, the Council urges priests to foster associations and social interactions among themselves in order to find mutual support and to build up their fraternal relationship as priests. In the United States, this often comes in the form of support groups in which priests gather regularly for camaraderie, sharing and prayer. A recent study conducted by the Seminary Department of the National Catholic Educational Association, *Grace Under Pressure: What Gives Life to American Priests* (36-37), confirms the experienced value of support groups among the "effective priests" interviewed for the study.

Other associations are also available. Often, for example, newly ordained priests are invited to join a group that consists of others who have been ordained only a few years. Sometimes, a diocese will connect the newly ordained with a more seasoned priest in a mentoring relationship. These arrangements can be important helps to a young priest in making the transition into full-time priestly ministry. The *Jesu Caritas* movement, another example, involves a more structured arrangement than a regular support group might, including a commitment not only to gather together regularly but also to spend an hour in prayer before the

Blessed Sacrament. The National Federation of Priests' Councils (NFPC) is an example of a larger national association that serves the interests and needs of priests.

In a particular way, the Council urges priests to attend especially to brother priests "who are laboring under difficulties—offering assistance, challenging them discretely, treating them with charity and compassion, and praying for them" (PO 8). Interestingly, Pope John Paul reiterates this teaching but goes on to extend this solicitude to priests no longer active in ministry (PDV 74).

Challenges and Obstacles

There are certainly a number of contemporary challenges and obstacles to realizing the priestly fraternity so beautifully symbolized in the ordination rite: With fewer priests, it is now more likely that priests will be living alone. Even if there are a number of nearby parishes, they are likely also to have only one priest. Other priests with whom a priest might wish to recreate and relax are therefore more likely to be at a distance. Certainly, related to the priest shortage, is the fact that the demands on the time and energy of the priest in a multifaceted contemporary parish can take up a good deal of the priest's life. Differing ecclesial views and theological viewpoints can separate priests who might otherwise have found it easier to associate with one another comfortably. Finally, some of the events that used to bring priests together have fallen by the wayside in some places, e.g., Forty Hours.

Accepting the Invitation

God will do the work; other priests will help. But in the end, all we can do is our own part in fostering a spirit of priestly fraternity within a presbyterate. We all certainly have known holy, effective and inspiring priests who have supported, encouraged and challenged us by their example. For that, we should be grateful. On the other hand, all of us have also known priests who have irritated, discouraged and even scandalized us. And this we should give over to God in prayer so that we can have courage to challenge others where appropriate, grace to forgive, and a firm resolve to learn from the attitudes and behaviors that have discouraged us in some way.

The challenge for each of us, as priests, is to strive ourselves to live the demands of being part of a priestly brotherhood and so become the kinds of priests who can offer to others the witness that holy priests have given to us. As the *Directory* (27) says:

> He will therefore make every effort to avoid living his own priesthood in an isolated and subjectivistic way, and he must try to enhance fraternal communion in the giving and receiving—from priest to priest—of the warmth of friendship, of affectionate help, of acceptance of fraternal correction, well aware that the grace of Orders "assumes and elevates human relations, psychologically, affectionately, cordially and spiritually."

As priests, we share with our bishop and our brother priests (as they actually are and not as we would want them to be) the task of continuing the mission of Jesus to spread the Good News and to gather the People of God together into the family of God. As much as possible, we ourselves should witness the unity of the family of God by witnessing unity with our brother priests. But, in the end, we must entrust them, our common mission and our own ministry to God—and simply do our part.

Seven

With and for the People of God

Introduction:

"1. The ordination of a priest should take place on a Sunday or holyday, when a large number of the faithful can attend....

"2. The ordination should take place ordinarily at the *cathedra* or bishop's chair; or, to enable the faithful to participate more fully, a chair for the bishop may be placed before the altar or elsewhere. A seat for the one to be ordained should be placed so that the faithful may have a complete view of the liturgical rites."

Presentation of the Candidate:

"Most Reverend Father, holy mother Church asks you to ordain this man, our brother, for service as priest."

"Do you judge him to be worthy?"

"After inquiry among the people of Christ and upon recommendation of those concerned with his training, I testify that he has been found worthy."

Election by the Bishop and Consent of the People, instructions:

"All present say: Thanks be to God, or give assent to the choice in some other way, according to local custom."

Homily, paragraph 8:

"Remember that you are chosen from among God's people and appointed to act for them in relation to God."

Examination, question 4:

"Are you resolved to consecrate your life to God for the salvation of his people...?"

Presentation of the Gifts:

"Accept from the holy people of God the gifts to be offered to him. Know what you are doing, and imitate the mystery you celebrate: model your life on the mystery of the Lord's cross."

* * *

The rite of ordination of a priest makes clear that the People of God have an important place in the ordination celebration and ultimately in the ordinand's future ministry as a priest. The rite calls for a "large number of the faithful" to be present, and it seeks to promote their participation in the rite, most practically by insuring that they can see the principal actions of the rite. The ordination will go forward after it has been attested that People of God have been consulted about the worthiness of the candidate for Orders. And, while the American custom of applauding often takes on the spirit of recognizing an accomplishment (like graduating or winning a prize), the rite makes clear that the People of God are asked for their consent to the ordination. (The rite itself suggests that the assembly say "Thanks be to God." In the Orthodox rite, the people acclaim "*Axios!*" [Worthy!])

In sum, the rite makes evident that the act of ordination is not simply a matter between the bishop (and his presbyterate) and the ordinand. The people have an important place in the rite, as they do in the ministerial priesthood of the ordained, and as they will in the actual exercise of the ordinand's priestly ministry.

The Ministerial Priesthood Serves the Common Priesthood

The Second Vatican Council teaches that the "priesthood of all believers" and "the priesthood of the ordained"—the "common" priesthood and "ordained" priesthood—are essentially different but ordered to one another. We are ordained priests in order to shape, to serve, to empower, to support the "spiritual sacrifice" of our brothers and sisters by which they live their share in the priesthood of Christ.

As ordained priests, we are leaders of the People of God, but we are leaders precisely in our service of *their* priestly self-offering. As Pope John Paul II has said, priesthood is a gift of Christ to the Church, for the service of the Church (*Holy Thursday* 1979:4). In the end, the priesthood of the ordained can only be understood in relation to its service to the priesthood of the People of God. The two ways of participating in the priesthood of Jesus Christ are, as the Council says, "ordered to one another."

Ordained service to the People of God, therefore, must begin with a profound sense of respect for the people we serve through our pastoral leadership (PO 9). It begins with a sense of being, first, fellow disciples sharing in a common faith and baptism. It is carried out in a spirit of service; it seeks to promote the dignity and the legitimate role of the laity in Church and society. It attends to their desires and advice; it seeks to enable their responses to the universal call to holiness; it is directed to their unity in charity. And so, the *Directory* (30) challenges priests to act in a respectful manner in our dealings with the people:

Therefore, he will exercise his spiritual mission with kindness and firmness, with humility and service, opening himself to compassion, participating in the sufferings which arise from the various forms of poverty, spiritual and material, old and new. He will know also how to act with humility and mercy within the difficult and uncertain ways of the conversion of sinners, to which he will exercise the gift of truth and patience and the encouraging benevolence of the Good Shepherd, who does not reprove the lost sheep, but carries it on his shoulders and celebrates for its return to the fold. (cf. Lk. 15:4-7)

In Persona Ecclesiae, In Persona Christi

As priests, we stand shoulder to shoulder *with* the People of God at the same time that we are set apart by Christ for a special ministry *for* the People of God. As priests, leaders of the People of God, we can be said to function *in persona ecclesiae* ("in the person of the Church," on behalf of the Church). The call to priesthood comes from within the Church; and the fact that the people are asked to give consent and that inquiry is made among them about the worthiness of a candidate for Orders indicates that they are part of the discernment of the call. Our personal faith was given to us through the Church, nurtured by our membership in the Church, enriched by the living tradition of the Church. Any true vocation is surely best nurtured in such fertile ground.

As priests, we proclaim and break open the Word of God, which is not our personal possession but the treasure of the entire People of God. We bring *their* gifts to the altar (as we did on the day of our ordination); we speak the great prayer of eucharistic remembering on *their* behalf; we speak the prayers *for them*, prayers that find root in *their* hearts, prayers that the *Church* raises to God. As the ordination homily says: "Remember that you are chosen from among God's people and appointed to act for them in relation to God."

Yet ultimately, priests function *in persona ecclesiae* (in the person of the Church) because we first function *in persona Christi capitis* (in the person of Christ as Head). Our call (certainly a good part of our discernment) comes *through* the Church, but fundamentally the call comes *from Christ* through the action of the bishop for the sake of the Church. And we are empowered to act *in persona ecclesiae*—on behalf of the People of God—because Christ has configured us to himself as Head and Shepherd of his people, to act *in persona Christi capitis*. And so, we are mediators; men "who stand between"; men consecrated to God by God's call—for the salvation of his people—as the ordination examination says.

Shaped by the People of God

In fact, the actual shape of our priesthood is molded in an important way by the actual communities that we have served, through positive experiences but also (and perhaps most especially) through the difficult times. Our gifts for ministry have been shaped by the support, the encouragement, the praise that we have received from the People of God: we are better preachers and teachers and shepherds and priests because of the ways, explicitly and implicitly, the people in our communities have reacted to us, affirmed us and challenged us.

Our ministry as priests has been powerfully shaped by the ways that the People of God have allowed us to be present in their lives: in the precious moments of birth and of dying, moments of failure and doubt and disappointment as well as moments of triumph and joy and success, moments of sin and of grace in the relationships that are nearest and dearest and most precious to them.

Even the difficulties, the obstacles, the struggles that we have encountered in our ministry have the potential of making us better Christians, better ministers, better priests. Certainly many priests know the experience of growing in their own priesthood and their own personal surrender to God in such difficult situations as closing or merging parishes, renovating church spaces, facing difficult conflict in the parish or within the pastoral staff. Of course, such challenges (like all of the difficulties of life) have the potential to make us bitter and cynical, more controlling, less trusting of others, less willing to give of ourselves generously ("stick our necks out" by investing ourselves in our ministries) *or* they can be invitations to surrender all to God, to trust in him, and simply to continue giving of ourselves generously in our daily ministerial responsibilities, knowing that God will work it out in the end.

Certainly, all of us have benefitted from the edifying witness of so many of the people for whom we have been priest. We all can think of the often simple but strong faith of the people who come to daily Mass day in and day out, the humility of the people who come to the confessional to lay open their sins before the Lord, the dedication of the people who take time out of *their* busy lives to volunteer to serve brothers and sisters in need—in their own parishes and beyond.

We have all been edified by the amazing faith of people who in the midst of great suffering, of great loss, of great pain have given testimony *to us* of the power of faith to endure. (So much can this be the case that we might sometimes ask: who was really ministering to whom?) We have all been touched by the wonderful hospitality of people who invite us into their homes, into their lives, into families and relationships.

The People of God do so much for us; the privilege of being priest to them enriches our lives so greatly. They can be such a support to us in our ministry and in our lives (and some of them can be our closest friends). In fact, the priests interviewed for *Grace Under Pressure* (pp. 38-43) indicated that friendships with lay men and women were truly life-giving for them. But the fact remains that we are *for* the People of God and not the other way around.

A priest is, as Jesus was (in the famous phrase of German theologian Dietrich Bonhoeffer), a "man for others." Surely those who are "specially configured" to him in order to represent him and to make him present in their lives and ministry must also be "men for others." Priests are men who have been set apart for service. We *are* servant-leaders—shepherds who give our lives for our people. This is not simply what we *do*; it is our identity, who and what we simply are.

The People of God can affirm us; they can support us; they can cheer and challenge and comfort us. And many of them do—and some of them do quite often—and some of them can become good friends. But most basically, we are *for them*, and not they for us. If we expect them primarily to comfort us in our sorrow, support us in our challenges, encourage us in our difficulties, the danger is that we will not attend, as the shepherds that we are, to *their* sorrows, to the challenges that *they* face; to the difficulties that *they* experience in their lives.

The danger is that, if we live for their affirmation, we could never challenge them as the authentic shepherd must, as the Word of God which we speak surely does, as the path to holiness for which we are guides requires, for fear that we might lose their affirmation.

If we look principally to them to cheer us, the danger is that they will be so busy giving *us* good cheer that they will mask their own pain. If we are not honest with ourselves in seeking from them relief from *our* occasional loneliness, the danger is that we'll cross boundaries that we ought not to cross— boundaries that protect us and our integrity, boundaries that protect them (and us) from hurt and shame and scandal. Good, solid relationships with lay people and even with parishioners are most certainly possible. I am only cautioning against a spirit or an attitude in which our motives (which are almost always a mix of good and bad) are really more self-serving than genuinely other-directed.

The fact is that most of us priests are generous and caring and anxious to minister to the Lord's precious people. But we are also sinners, which means that we are always capable of selfishness, of self-serving, of self-aggrandizement. We are all too capable of using our authority, our sacred status, and sometimes our power to defend ourselves, to put others down, to make ourselves feel good about ourselves, in short, to serve ourselves rather than truly serving others.

Any action, pattern or relationship that is principally self-serving ought not to be, because we are shepherds and ministers of the Word of God and priestly sanctifiers of the People of God. We don't just *perform* pastoral actions; we don't just *say* holy words; we don't simply *do* sacred things. We *are* shepherds; we *are* preachers; we *are* priests. We simply *are* "men for others" at the core of our being and at the heart of our identity—at every moment of our lives, whatever we are doing, whomever we are with.

Human, sinful and possessing every need that our sisters and brothers possess, we are nonetheless *fundamentally* men *for others*, men *for* the People of God. We are men whose lives have been consecrated to God for the salvation of his people, as the examination in the ordination rite asks us to affirm, and to which each one of us has said: "I am, with the help of God."

Eight

In a Priestly Way of Life

Homily, paragraph 5:

"Meditate on the law of God, believe what you read, teach what you believe, and put into practice what you teach."

Homily, paragraph 6:

"Let the example of your life attract the followers of Christ, so that by word and action you may build up the house which is God's Church."

Homily, paragraph 7:

"Know what you are doing and imitate the mystery you celebrate. In the memorial of the Lord's death and resurrection, make every effort to die to sin and to walk in the new life of Christ."

Homily, paragraph 8:

"Do your part in the work of Christ the Priest with genuine joy and love, and attend to the concerns of Christ before your own."

Homily, paragraph 9:

"Always remember the example of the Good Shepherd who came not to be served but to serve, and to seek out and rescue those who were lost."

Examination, question 4:

"Are you resolved to consecrate your life to God for the salvation of his people, and to unite yourself more closely every day to Christ the High Priest, who offered himself for us to the Father as a perfect sacrifice?"

Promise of Obedience:

"May God who has begun the good work in you bring it to fulfillment."

Litany of the Saints:

"In your sight we offer this man for ordination: support him with your unfailing love."

Prayer of Consecration:

"Renew within him the Spirit of holiness. As a co-worker with the order of bishops may he be faithful to the ministry that he receives from you, Lord God, and be to others a model of right conduct."

Presentation of Gifts:

"Know what you are doing, and imitate the mystery you celebrate: model your life on the mystery of the Lord's cross."

* * *

The ordination homily that appears as a sample in the rite of ordination follows closely the theology of priesthood that is laid out in *Presbyterorum Ordinis* (*The Decree on the Ministry and Life of Priests*) of the Second Vatican Council: the priest acting in the name and person of Jesus Christ as Head continues and shares in the mission of Jesus as Preacher/Teacher, Shepherd and Priest. But the homily doesn't merely *define* the priesthood for the sake of the ordinand and congregation like a theological lecture. The homily, in each case, challenges the ordinand to live faithfully the reality of what he is to become by ordination.

According to the homily, in the life of the priest, one's whole life is to be conformed to one's sacred functions. The challenge is to become what we proclaim we are, what we said we would become on the day of our ordination. We are men chosen in the mysterious and wonderful plan of God to be specially configured to Christ, to continue his mission as Teacher, as Pastor and as Priest—teaching, pastoring and sanctifying. But that ministry can only be carried out effectively if our actions, the example of our lives, the unspoken testimony of the way we live, also teaches and guides and leads others to holiness, in their surrender to God (see PDV 24-25).

We strive to become ever more conformed to Christ whom we represent, in whose person and name we act, to whom we have been specially configured. To be ever more closely conformed to Christ requires drawing ever closer to him in prayer, learning to know him better through regular encounter with his Word, and by modeling in our own lives his pattern of self-giving. (And it requires, too, that those who serve as confessors also regularly come to the sacrament of Reconciliation as penitents, seeking the grace of forgiveness and of ongoing conversion so that our lives can be ever more authentically conformed to Christ.)

In Christ, our High Priest, our lives as priests have to be surrendered to God for the sake of the people, given over to God in service of the people. As one of the questions in the examination says: "Are you resolved to consecrate your life to God for the salvation of his people, and to unite yourself more closely every day to Christ the High Priest, who offered himself for us to the Father as a perfect sacrifice?" We must become, like Jesus, more and more "a man for others" because, like him, we are, first of all, "men of God."

In short, as both the Council (PO 14) and Pope John Paul II (PDV 23) teach, pastoral charity must become the integrating principle of the priest's life—his plans, his projects, and his priorities subordinated to, organized around, in conformity with the love he has, as a shepherd, for the people. Our love for God, which we share with every Christian, must be—for ourselves *as priests*—expressed in our love for the flock. For many of the Fathers of the Church, this was made clear in the post-resurrection appearance of Jesus recorded in the Gospel of John (21:15-16): "Simon, son of John, do you love me? Feed my sheep." Every priest is told: if you love me, feed my sheep.

But to be conformed to Christ means that, more and more, we must depend on him, we must trust in him, we must wait on him—not on things that we can possess, people we can control, status we can attain, accomplishments we can parade before others. And, in the struggles, the challenges, the doubts, the temptations we encounter in our ministry, we must allow ourselves to hear from him what St. Paul heard from him when he prayed that the thorn in his flesh might be taken away: "My grace is enough for you" (2 Cor. 12:9). My grace is enough for you.

And, of course inescapably, conformity to Christ in the priestly life means prayer—prayer though there are a million things to do, prayer *because* there are a million things to do. We must pray for ourselves, pray for our ministry, pray for the people entrusted to our care, pray for no other reason than that a God so full of gratuitous love deserves it.

Our ministry as priests is ultimately and most truly Christ's ministry lived in us. When we baptize, it is Christ who baptizes;

when we reconcile, it is Christ who reconciles. When we proclaim the Gospel, it is he who speaks; when we preside at Eucharist, it is really Christ who presides (SC 7).

Many of the priests interviewed for *Grace Under Pressure* (pp. 57-59) reported the "mysterious" ways that the People of God had felt touched by their words or actions—far beyond what the priest himself could have imagined, and perhaps without the priest even being aware that he had done anything to be of help. It is Christ who acts in us, and he has power to empower, to transform and to far exceed anything that we could intend even by the best of our actions.

What an awesome and humbling thought: Christ Jesus— Savior, Redeemer, Son of God—acts in me, speaks in my words! More and more, then, in our lives and ministry, it must be as John the Baptizer says in the Gospel of John: "He must increase, while I must decrease" (Jn. 3:30), until we can say with St. Paul: "I live now, not I, but Christ lives in me" (Gal. 2:20).

Our daily priestly ministry ought to change our lives— slowly, over time (of course!). How could it be otherwise when Christ acts in us, while we can see how very far our own lives are from being like his? At every Eucharist (and at how many Eucharists does the typical priest preside on a Sunday, during a single week, sometimes on a single day?), the priest says "This is my Body which will be given up for you." Yes, these are the words of Christ which we speak in his name and in his person. But how could we say these words almost every day of our lives and not hear the challenge in them for one who acts in his name and in his person (Greshake, 113)? "This is my Body which is given up for you." As the Council says (PO 13), "So when priests unite themselves with the act of Christ the Priest they daily offer themselves to God, and being nourished with Christ's Body they share in the charity of him who gives himself as food to the faithful."

In the Prayer of Consecration in the rite of ordination, the bishop first recalls the ways that God has called forth helpers to carry on his work, and the bishop asks God to give him helpers as God has done in the past. Yet the first prayer directed to the ordinand kneeling before the bishop says: "Almighty Father, grant to this servant of yours the dignity of the priesthood. Renew within him the Spirit of holiness."

Renew within Him the Spirit of holiness. Pope John Paul says (PDV 27): "The Holy Spirit poured out in the Sacrament of Holy Orders is a source of holiness and a call to sanctification." And the priest's holiness will be found precisely in his ministry: "Priests will acquire holiness in their own distinctive way by exercising their functions sincerely and tirelessly in the Spirit of Christ" (PO 13). The challenge and the invitation and commitment that we accepted on the day of our ordination calls out to each of us—ever more faithfully, ever more consistently, ever more authentically—to become men whose lives are firmly set on the path to holiness, guides on the path of holiness for the People of God, holy men according to the distinctive holiness of priests: united with Christ the Shepherd in the self-giving love of a shepherd for his sheep.

A Select Bibliography

Barron, Robert E. "Priest as Bearer of the Mystery." *Church 10* (Summer 1994): 10-13.

Crichton, J.D. *Christian Celebration: Understanding the Sacraments*. Third edition. London: Geoffrey Chapman, 1993.

Dulles, Avery. *The Priestly Office: A Theological Reflection*. New York: Paulist, 1997.

Greshake, Gisbert. *The Meaning of the Christian Priesthood*. Dublin: Four Courts, 1988.

Hume, Basil. *Light in the Lord: Reflections on the Priesthood*. Collegeville, MN: Liturgical Press, 1993.

Jounel, Pierre. "Ordinations." In *The Church At Prayer: An Introduction to the Liturgy*, Vol. III: *The Sacraments*. Edited by Aimé Georges Martimort. New edition. Collegeville, MN: Liturgical Press, 1988.

O'Keefe, Mark. *In Persona Christi: Reflections on Priestly Identity and Holiness*. St. Meinrad, IN: Abbey Press, 1998.

Walsh, James, et al. *Grace Under Pressure: What Gives Life to American Priests (A Study of Effective Priests Ordained Ten to Thirty Years)*. Washington, DC: National Catholic Educational Association, 1995.

Appendix

ORDINATION OF A PRIEST

INTRODUCTION

1. The ordination of a priest should take place on a Sunday or holyday, when a large number of the faithful can attend, unless pastoral reasons suggest another day.

2. The ordination should take place ordinarily at the *cathedra* or bishop's chair; or, to enable the faithful to participate more fully, a chair for the bishop may be placed before the altar or elsewhere. A seat for the one to be ordained should be placed so that the faithful may have a complete view of the liturgical rites.

3. The priest concelebrates with the bishop in his ordination Mass. It is most appropriate for the bishop to admit other priests to the concelebration; in this case and on this day the newly ordained priest takes the first place ahead of the others who concelebrate.

4. The one to be ordained wears an alb (with an amice and cincture unless other provisions are made) and a deacon's stole. In addition to what is needed for the concelebration of Mass, there should be ready: (a) the Roman Pontifical; (b) stoles for the priests who lay hands upon the candidate; (c) a chasuble for the candidate; (d) a linen gremial; (e) holy chrism; (f) whatever is needed for the washing of hands.

5. When everything is ready, the procession moves through the church to the altar in the usual way. A deacon carries the Book of the Gospels; he is followed by the candidate then the concelebrating priests, and finally the bishop between two deacons.

LITURGY OF THE WORD

6. The liturgy of the word takes place according to the rubrics.

7. The readings may be taken in whole or in part from the Mass of the day or from the texts listed in Chapter VI.

8. The profession of faith is not said, nor are the general intercessions.

ORDINATION OF A PRIEST

9. The ordination of a priest begins after the gospel. The bishop, wearing his miter, sits at his chair.

CALLING OF THE CANDIDATE

10. The candidate is called by the deacon:
Let N. who is to be ordained priest please come forward.

11. The candidate answers: **Present,** and goes to the bishop, before whom he makes a sign of reverence.

PRESENTATION OF THE CANDIDATE

12. When the candidate is in his place before the bishop, the priest designated by the bishop says:

Most Reverend Father, holy mother Church asks you to ordain this man, our brother, for service as priest.

The bishop asks:
Do you judge him to be worthy?

He answers:
After inquiry among the people of Christ and upon

recommendation of those concerned with his training, I testify that he has been found worthy.

ELECTION BY THE BISHOP AND CONSENT OF THE PEOPLE

13. Bishop:

We rely on the help of the Lord God and our Savior Jesus Christ, and we choose this man, our brother, for priesthood in the presbyteral order.

All present say: **Thanks be to God,** or give their assent to the choice in some other way, according to local custom.

HOMILY

14. Then all sit, and the bishop addresses the people and the candidate on the duties of a priest. He may use these words:

This man, your relative and friend, is now to be raised to the order of priests. Consider carefully the position to which he is to be promoted in the Church.

It is true that God has made his entire people a royal priesthood in Christ. But our High Priest, Jesus Christ, also chose some of his followers to carry out publicly in the Church a priestly ministry in his name on behalf of mankind. He was sent by the Father, and he in turn sent the apostles into the world; through them and their successors, the bishops, he continues his work as Teacher, Priest, and Shepherd. Priests are co-workers of the order of bishops. They are joined to the bishops in the priestly office and are called to serve God's people.

Our brother has seriously considered this step and is now to be ordained to priesthood in the presbyteral order. He is to

serve Christ the Teacher, Priest, and Shepherd in his ministry which is to make his own body, the Church, grow into the people of God, a holy temple.

He is called to share in the priesthood of the bishops and to be molded into the likeness of Christ, the supreme and eternal Priest. By consecration he will be made a true priest of the New Testament, to preach the Gospel, sustain God's people, and celebrate the liturgy, above all, the Lord's sacrifice.

He then addresses the candidate:

My son, you are now to be advanced to the order of the presbyterate. You must apply your energies to the duty of teaching in the name of Christ, the chief Teacher. Share with all mankind the word of God you have received with joy. Meditate on the law of God, believe what you read, teach what you believe, and put into practice what you teach.

Let the doctrine you teach be true nourishment for the people of God. Let the example of your life attract the followers of Christ, so that by word and action you may build up the house which is God's Church.

In the same way you must carry out your mission of sanctifying in the power of Christ. Your ministry will perfect the spiritual sacrifice of the faithful by uniting it to Christ's sacrifice, the sacrifice which is offered sacramentally through your hands. Know what you are doing and imitate the mystery you celebrate. In the memorial of the Lord's death and resurrection, make every effort to die to sin and to walk in the new life of Christ.

When you baptize, you will bring men and women into the people of God. In the sacrament of penance, you will forgive sins in the name of Christ and the Church. With holy oil you will relieve and console the sick. You will celebrate the liturgy and offer thanks and praise to God throughout the day, praying not only for the people of God but for the whole world. Remember that you are chosen from among God's people and appointed to act for them in relation to God. Do your part in the work of Christ the Priest with genuine joy and love, and attend to the concerns of Christ before your own.

Finally, conscious of sharing in the work of Christ, the Head and Shepherd of the Church, and united with the bishop and subject to him, seek to bring the faithful together into a unified family and to lead them effectively, through Christ and in the Holy Spirit, to God the Father. Always remember the example of the Good Shepherd who came not to be served but to serve, and to seek out and rescue those who were lost.

EXAMINATION OF THE CANDIDATE

15. The candidate then stands before the bishop, who questions him:

My son, before you proceed to the order of the presbyterate, declare before the people your intention to undertake this priestly office.

Are you resolved, with the help of the Holy Spirit, to discharge without fail the office of priesthood in the presbyteral order as a conscientious fellow worker with the bishops in caring for the Lord's flock?
The candidate answers: I am.

Bishop:
Are you resolved to celebrate the mysteries of Christ faithfully and religiously as the Church has handed them down to us for the glory of God and the sanctification of Christ's people?

Candidate: **I am.**

Bishop:
Are you resolved to exercise the ministry of the word worthily and wisely, preaching the Gospel and explaining the Catholic faith?
Candidate: **I am.**

Bishop:
Are you resolved to consecrate your life to God for the salvation of his people, and to unite yourself more closely every day to Christ the High Priest, who offered himself for us to the Father as a perfect sacrifice?
Candidate: **I am, with the help of God.**

PROMISE OF OBEDIENCE

16. Then the candidate goes to the bishop and, kneeling before him, places his joined hands between those of the bishop. If this gesture seems less suitable in some places, the conference of bishops may choose another gesture or sign.

If the bishop is the candidate's own Ordinary, he asks:
Do you promise respect and obedience to me and my successors?
Candidate: **I do.**

If the bishop is not the candidate's own Ordinary, he asks:
Do you promise respect and obedience to your Ordinary?
Candidate: **I do.**

Bishop:
May God who has begun the good work in you bring it to fulfillment.

INVITATION TO PRAYER

17. Then all stand, and the bishop, without his miter, invites the people to pray:

My dear people, let us pray, that the all-powerful Father may pour out the gifts of heaven on this servant of his, whom he has chosen to be a priest.

Deacon (except during the Easter season):
Let us kneel.

LITANY OF THE SAINTS

18. The candidate prostrates himself and, except during the Easter season, the rest kneel at their places.

The cantors begin the litany (see Chapter VI); they may add, at the proper place, names of other saints (for example, the patron saint, the titular of the church, the founder of the church, the patron saint of the one to be ordained) or petitions suitable to the occasion.

19. The bishop alone stands and, with his hands joined, sings or says:

**Hear us, Lord our God,
and pour out upon this servant of yours
the blessing of the Holy Spirit
and the grace and power of the priesthood.
In your sight we offer this man for ordination:
support him with your unfailing love.**

**We ask this through Christ our Lord.
R. Amen.**

Deacon: **Let us stand.**

LAYING ON OF HANDS

20. Then all stand. The candidate goes to the bishop and kneels before him. The bishop lays his hands on the candidate's head, in silence.

21. Next all the priests present, wearing stoles, lay their hands upon the candidate in silence. After the laying on of hands, the priests remain on either side of the bishop until the prayer of consecration is completed.

PRAYER OF CONSECRATION

22. The candidate kneels before the bishop. With his hands extended over the candidate, the bishop sings the prayer of consecration or says it aloud:

Come to our help,
Lord, holy Father, almighty and eternal God;
you are the source of every honor and dignity,
of all progress and stability.
You watch over the growing family of man
by your gift of wisdom and your pattern of order.
When you had appointed high priests to rule
    your people,
you chose other men next to them in rank and dignity
to be with them and to help them in their task;
and so there grew up
the ranks of priests and the offices of levites,
established by sacred rites.

In the desert
you extended the spirit of Moses to seventy wise men
who helped him to rule the great company of his
    people.

You shared among the sons of Aaron
the fullness of their father's power,
to provide worthy priests in sufficient number
for the increasing rites of sacrifice and worship.
With the same loving care
you gave companions to your Son's apostles
to help in teaching the faith:
they preached the Gospel to the whole world.

Lord,
grant also to us such fellow workers,
for we are weak and our need is greater.

Almighty Father,
grant to this servant of yours
the dignity of the priesthood.
Renew within him the Spirit of holiness.
As a co-worker with the order of bishops
may he be faithful to the ministry
that he receives from you, Lord God,
and be to others a model of right conduct.

May he be faithful in working with the order of
    bishops,
so that the words of the Gospel may reach the ends of
    the earth,
and the family of nations,
made one in Christ,
may become God's one, holy people.

We ask this through our Lord Jesus Christ, your Son,
who lives and reigns with you and the Holy Spirit,
one God, for ever and ever.
R. Amen.

INVESTITURE WITH STOLE AND CHASUBLE

23. After the prayer of consecration, the bishop, wearing his miter, sits, and the newly ordained stands. The assisting priests return to their places, but one of them arranges the stole of the newly ordained as it is worn by priests and vests him in a chasuble.

ANOINTING OF HANDS

24. Next the bishop receives a linen gremial and anoints with chrism the palms of the new priest as he kneels before him. The bishop says:

The Father anointed our Lord Jesus Christ
through the power of the Holy Spirit.
May Jesus preserve you to sanctify the Christian
**   people**
and to offer sacrifice to God.

25. While the new priest is being vested in stole and chasuble and the bishop is anointing his hands, the hymn **Veni, Creator Spiritus** or the following antiphon may be sung with Psalm 110.

Christ the Lord,
a priest for ever in the line of Melchizedek,
offered bread and wine.

The antiphon is repeated after every two verses. **Glory to the Father** is not said. The psalm is interrupted and the antiphon repeated when the hands of the priest have been anointed.

Any other appropriate song may be sung.

Then the bishop and the new priest wash their hands.

PRESENTATION OF THE GIFTS

26. The deacon assists the bishop in receiving the gifts of the people and he prepares the bread on the paten and the wine and water in the chalice for the celebration of Mass. He brings the paten and chalice to the bishop, who hands them to the new priest as he kneels before him. The bishop says:

Accept from the holy people of God the gifts to be offered to him.
Know what you are doing, and imitate the mystery you celebrate:
model your life on the mystery of the Lord's cross.

KISS OF PEACE

27. Lastly, the bishop stands and gives the kiss of peace to the new priest, saying:

Peace be with you.

The priest responds: **And also with you.**

If circumstances permit, the priests present also give the kiss of peace to the newly ordained.

28. Meanwhile, the following antiphon may be sung with Psalm 100.

You are my friends, says the Lord, if you do what I command you.

The antiphon is repeated after every two verses. **Glory to the Father** is not said. The psalm is interrupted and the antiphon repeated when all have received the kiss of peace.

Any other appropriate song may be sung, or:

No longer do I call you servants, but my friends,

because you know all that I have done among you
(alleluia).
—Receive the Holy Spirit as an Advocate among you:
it is he whom the Father will send you (alleluia).
You are my friends if you do the things I command
you.
—Receive the Holy Spirit as an Advocate among you.
Glory to the Father...
—It is he whom the Father will send you (alleluia).

LITURGY OF THE EUCHARIST

29. The rite for the concelebration of Mass is followed with
these changes:
a) The preparation of the chalice is omitted.
b) In Eucharist Prayer I, the special form of **Father, accept this
offering** is said:

Father, accept this offering
from your whole family
and from the one you have chosen for the order of
    priests.
Protect the gifts you have given him,
and let him yield a harvest worthy of you.

[Through Christ our Lord. Amen.]